GRAPHOLOGY

A concise guide to the study of handwriting and what it can reveal about the hidden depths of character and personality.

By the same author
BIORHYTHMS
LIFE LINES: AN INTRODUCTION TO PALMISTRY

GRAPHOLOGY

Understanding What Handwriting Reveals

by

PETER WEST

THE AQUARIAN PRESS
Wellingborough, Northamptonshire

First published 1981
Second Impression 1984
Third Impression 1986

© PENTAGON 1981

British Library Cataloguing in Publication Data

West, Peter
    Graphology.
    1. Graphology
    1. Title
    137   BF891

    ISBN 0-85030-260-9

Printed and bound in Great Britain by
Richard Clay (The Chaucer Press) Ltd.,
Bungay, Suffolk.

CONTENTS

INTRODUCTION

One of the definitions of graphology is the study and analysis of handwriting for the purpose of interpreting character and personality. Graphological analyses are most commonly used for vocational guidance, personnel selection and pre-marital or marital compatibility.

No extra-sensory perception is required; one cannot foretell the future, although a graphologist may be able to predict the reactions of a particular writer with whose script he is familiar if and when certain conditions or circumstances arise. But this would require great experience and an in-depth study on the part of the graphologist; it is as well, therefore, for the student or amateur graphologist to regard the subject as a useful tool for assessing personality.

However, it should also be remembered that graphology is only one tool in determining an individual's character make-up and should be used in conjunction with other methods of assessment if a full and accurate analysis is required. For example, graphology cannot be utilized to detect the age of the writer, although it may be possible to discern great age or the writing of the very young; but even this can prove difficult. Also, the sex of a writer may not be obvious. It is now accepted that certain feminine traits can occur in the writing of a man and that a woman may exhibit masculine tendencies.

Basically, handwriting reflects the mood or thought processes *at the time of writing*. Therefore, the same person's handwriting will vary according to the way he or she feels at the time when the writing is executed: mood, health, speed, even the importance of the subject matter – all will have a bearing on the formation of the script.

A useful exercise for the student graphologist would be to write a few lines as you feel your mood change or, better still, to glance through your notes and observe changes of mood as your studies have progressed. In particular, if you look back to notes made at times when difficulties have been encountered, you should be able to spot the changes in your 'normal' handwriting at those times.

It is, however, beyond the scope of this book to enter into the deeper meanings and interpretations employed in psychological analysis. This book is intended as a simple, basic guide, an introduction to the fascinating world of graphology.

Requirements for Analysis

Ideally, a sample should be at least a hundred words in length, on a sheet of unlined paper, preferably at least 10″ x 8″, and should, wherever possible, include a signature.

The writer should use his normal pen, ballpoint or fountain, not a fibre tip and never a pencil. The text should not be copied from a book or magazine and should be in prose form, not poetry. Obviously, therefore, the ideal sample will be one which the writer has executed naturally – a recent letter for example – and not one which has been written specifically for the purposes of analysis.

When you begin your analysis, start at the end of the sample and work *towards the beginning*. This may sound like odd advice, but it isn't. Often, the sample has been written specifically for analysis and the writer may tend to be self-conscious at the beginning of his script but is likely to be less so as he proceeds with the text. Even a letter written to a friend tends to be more consciously executed at its commencement than at its termination: once the writer becomes more involved in the content or message of the communication he becomes less conscious of the manner in which he is forming his written words.

The Golden Rule

It is important to remember that each character trait revealed in a handwriting is only a clue and should not be regarded in isolation or as representing the sum total of the personality under consideration. An occasional sign may, for example, be exactly that: an occasional trend towards one particular characteristic. Also, all traits, clues and signs have both positive and negative aspects, and this facet, too, must be taken into account.

A disciplined graphologist will never jump to conclusions; he will observe and evaluate the entire sample very carefully, bearing in mind that it will always reflect the writer's mood at the time of writing. He may even take a pen himself and trace a line or word in order to determine how the writing was executed originally; he will learn to balance and counterbalance each facet of the script until he feels that he has a reasonable picture of the whole personality thus revealed. Then, and only then, does the experienced graphologist prepare his report.

CHAPTER ONE

THE WHOLE VIEW

When looking at an example of handwriting the whole view – the way the writing is laid out on the paper and the width of the margins – is the first thing one notices. One's attention is then given to the legibility, slope and consistency of the script itself.

Margins

Some people possess a good standard of visual perception which is reflected in the way they place their writing on the page. Their script is of even proportions and they adhere strictly to equal margins, indicating a reasonably meticulous approach and a good sense of symmetry and form. These subjects may be of above average intelligence and their cultural standards may also be high.

Such a high standard of presentation is not commonly encountered but, once seen, it is not forgotten because its effect is so pleasing (see *Figure 1*, overleaf).

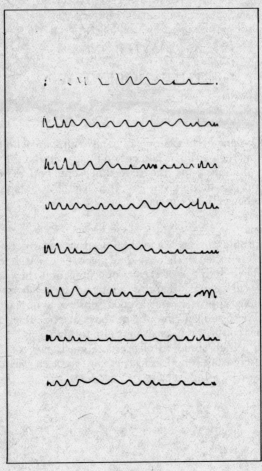

Figure 1.

A wide margin to the left-hand side of the paper indicates a basically friendly, considerate personality. These people may possess a certain amount of reserve in their overall personalities, although they are liable to display a tendency towards extravagance at times.

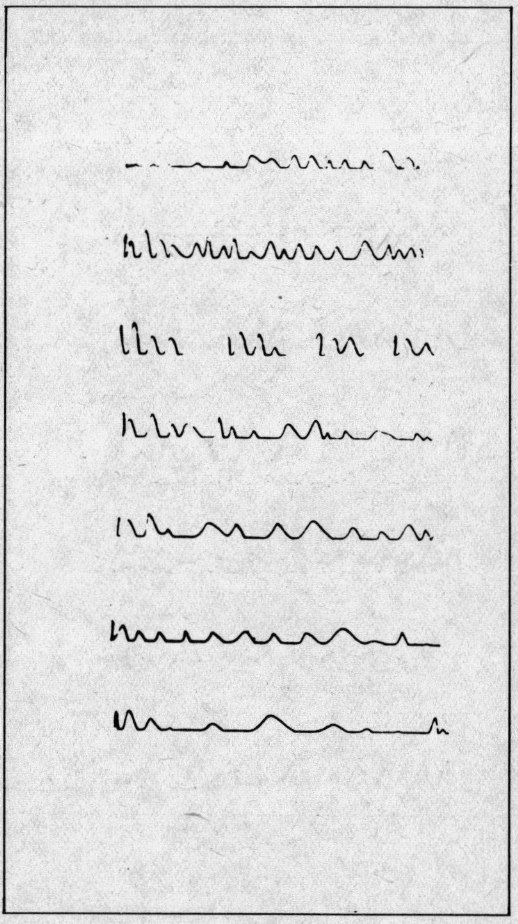

Figure 2.

When the right-hand margin is the wider, it shows the writer's concern with matters pertaining to future events. Not naturally a good mixer, such an individual may lack spontaneity of approach and response, underestimate his or her own capabilities and be unable to express himself well.

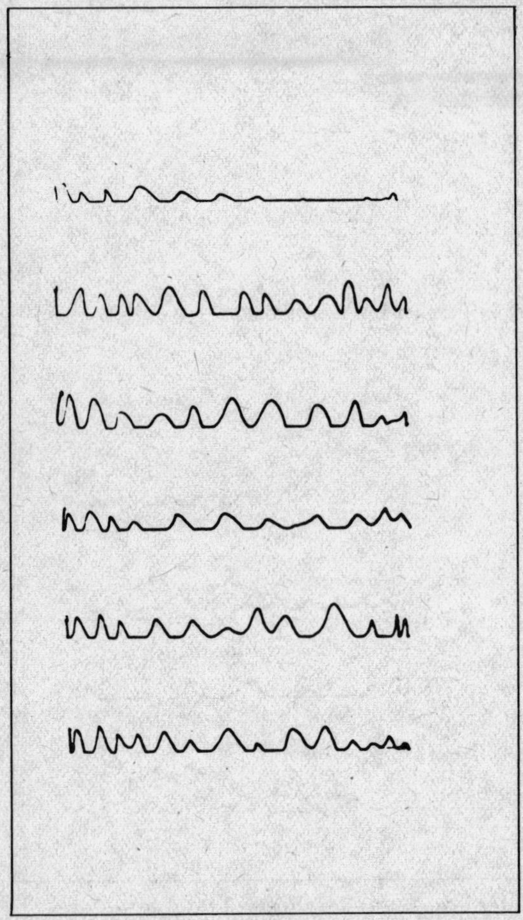

Figure 3.

When the margin to the top of the script is very wide it shows a tendency towards indifference. A writer who lays out his page in such a manner usually has a rather basic and matter-of-fact attitude towards other people and to life in general.

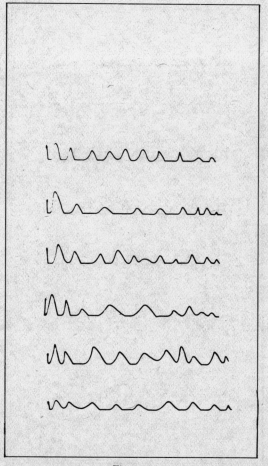

Figure 4.

A wide margin at the bottom of the page indicates poor planning ability and, sometimes, a general lack of forethought. Often this thoughtlessness is displayed in the subject's dealings with others and can result in misunderstandings and difficulties in relationships.

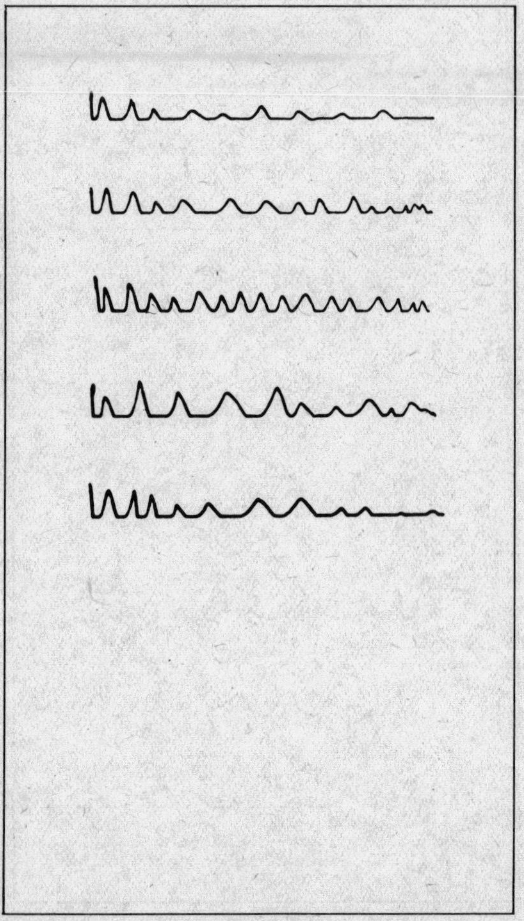

Figure 5.

A narrow right-hand margin is indicative of an inhibited nature. Impulsive and outspoken, enthusiastic and full of fun, such people can be a little over-emphatic at times. Despite this, however, they display strong, commonsense attitudes to problems although they sometimes tend to take short-cuts in solving them.

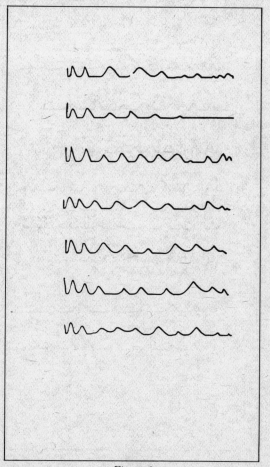

Figure 6.

It is quite usual for the right-hand margin of a handwriting sample to be the one which is uneven and untidy. Yet, although this may be regarded as the 'average', it does indicate a certain amount of lack of forethought in the personality.

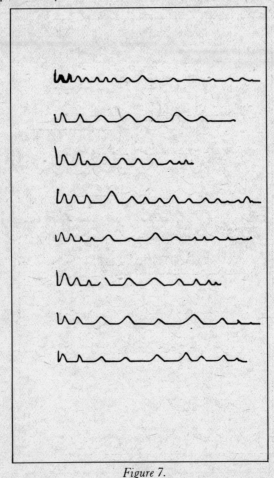

Figure 7.

An uneven left-hand margin, however, implies less control and a rather more spontaneous nature. These writers display little initial reserve in their dealings with others and their ideas flow smoothly and reasonably quickly.

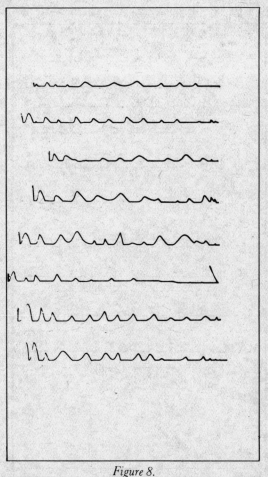

Figure 8.

A left-hand margin which becomes progressively narrower towards the bottom of the page indicates a concern with economy. These people have a tendency to stop and think about intended plans. They become increasingly cautious as projects progress and dislike making errors of any kind.

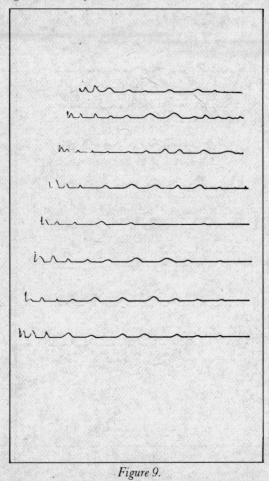

Figure 9.

When the left-hand margin widens increasingly from the top of the page to the bottom, however, it reveals the reverse of these traits. Such writers exhibit haste, impulsiveness and impatience. They may spend lavishly on gifts or luxuries and tend not to worry overmuch about costs generally.

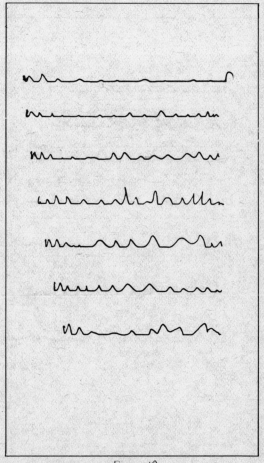

Figure 10.

Should the right-hand margin become increasingly narrow it implies that any initial shyness or reserve in the writer's personality will become less apparent with familiarity. These individuals tend to hold back a little of themselves at the start of a relationship, but soon lose this initial reticence.

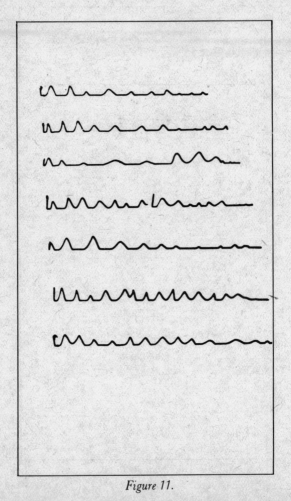

Figure 11.

A handwriting sample that almost fills the sheet of paper, leaving very narrow margins all round, indicates two almost conflicting personality traits. It can be an indication of stinginess, austerity and an acquisitive nature. Yet such people often display generosity towards charitable organizations and their acquisitiveness frequently manifests as an excessive fondness for luxuries.

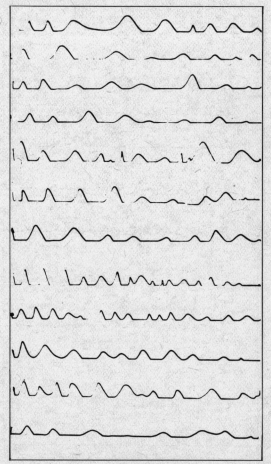

Figure 12.

Very wide margins all round the paper indicate a sense of isolation. These individuals usually appear aloof and reserved; they may withdraw from normal society and are often secretive about personal matters. Very often, of course, these traits lead to loneliness.

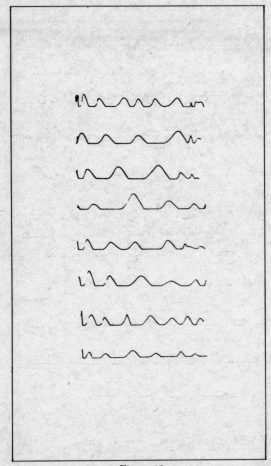

Figure 13.

Sometimes, but rarely, one encounters a handwriting sample where all the margins are irregular, indicative of carelessness and inattentiveness. However, such subjects, although disorganized, are usually quite versatile, adaptable and display tolerance, even when under criticism.

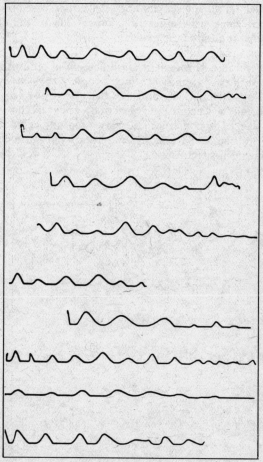

Figure 14.

Line Slope

One of the reasons why a handwriting sample should be executed on unlined paper is so that the graphologist can study the consistency of the lines of script. Sometimes the lines of writing slope up from or down to an imaginary, horizontal base-line; or perhaps the individual words are executed in an uneven manner. In either case, the line or word slope will represent another clue to the overall character analysis of the writer.

When the whole writing appears to slope or rise upward at the end of each line it is an indication of optimism and general inner contentment. Such people possess a marked degree of self-confidence and well-being, creating an overall impression of warmth and affection. They are not easily discouraged, do not remain depressed for long and have the ability to bounce back after any set-backs because of their strongly resilient natures.

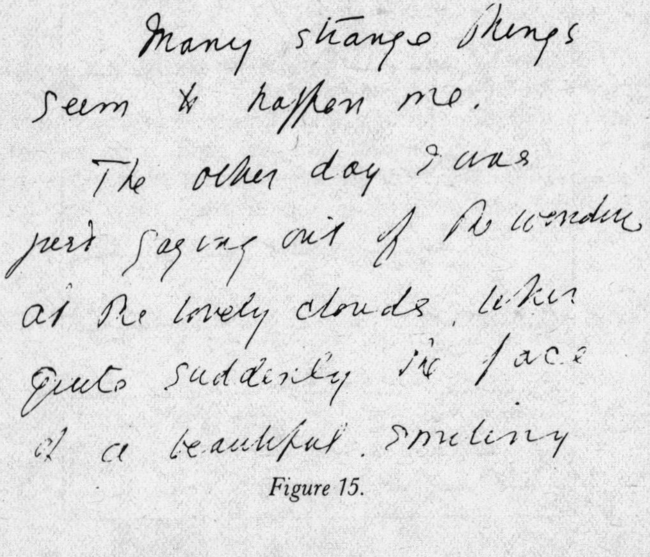

Figure 15.

Conversely, downward sloping handwriting is indicative of opposing tendencies. These writers display pessimism and despondency and may remain discouraged for longer than is good for them: sometimes to the extent of affecting their physical well-being. Indeed, this style of writing is frequently encountered when the subject is currently weighed down with problems or is physically tired.

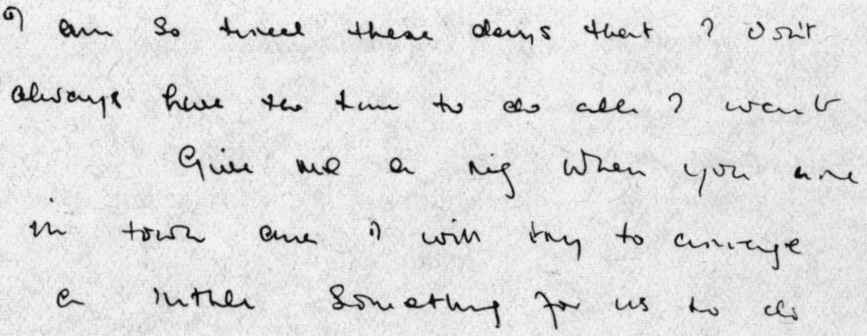

Figure 16.

Consistently horizontal lines of handwriting indicate a reliable, even-tempered, self-controlled nature. Although such people may appear dull and uninteresting, they possess a marked degree of resolution and good, solid reasoning powers; these are the people whom others turn to when they have problems to solve or routine tasks that they want completed.

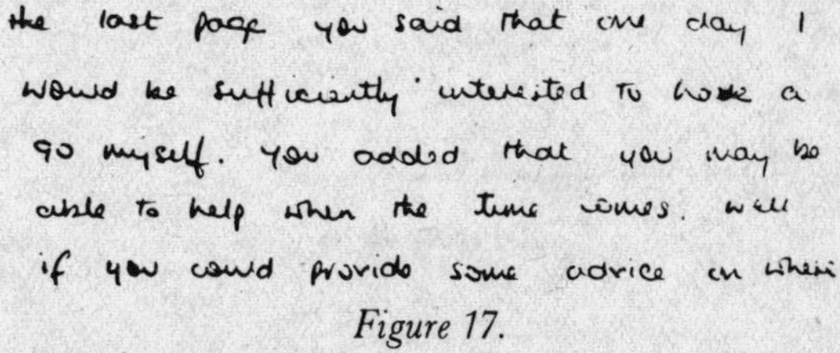

Figure 17.

Sometimes the whole writing appears to bow or arch in the centre: each line rises at its commencement but slopes down at the end, forming a definite arc. These writers begin projects with great verve but usually quickly lose interest once their initial enthusiasm has waned. They soon grow bored with their many and varied enterprises and consequently seldom complete them.

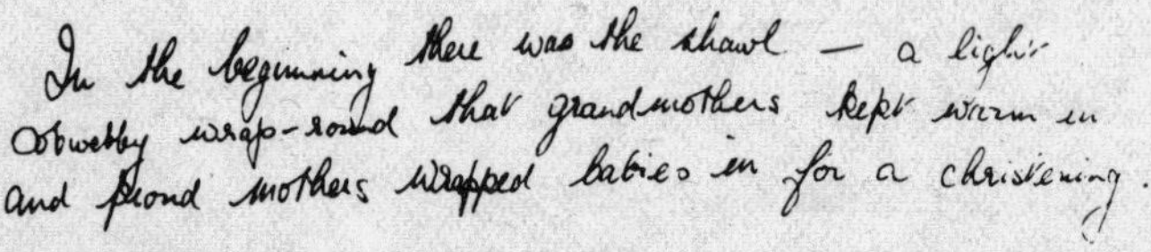

In the beginning there was the shawl — a light cobwebby wrap-round that grandmothers kept warm in and proud mothers wrapped babies in for a christening.

Figure 18.

The reverse line formation, a dished or concave effect, implies the reverse personality type. This is the individual who approaches each project with extreme caution and slight misgivings, but who becomes increasingly enthusiastic and optimistic about the eventual outcome as the scheme or plan progresses. Slow starters, these writers see their undertakings through.

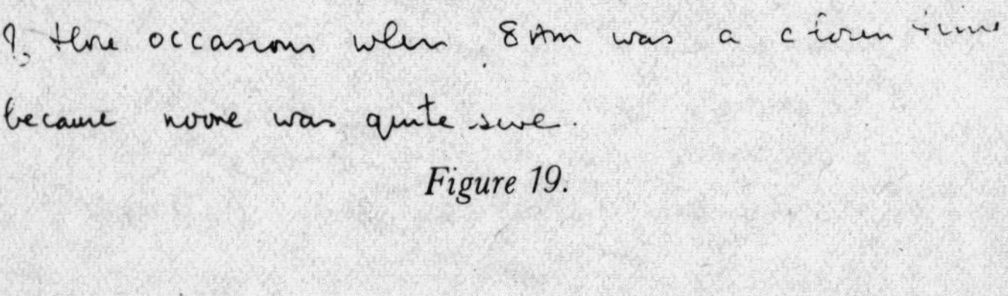

me whether Sam is accurate or whether ten is one 9, there occasions when Sam was a ciurm time because noone was quite sure.

Figure 19.

Word Slope

A handwriting sample sometimes appears quite even at first glance, each line following a horizontal course across the page. However, on closer examination it may become apparent that each word is executed in a sloping manner despite the overall visual evenness of the lines of script.

When each word descends it implies a lack of self-confidence on the part of the writer. Such people need constant reassurance and encouragement and, if these are not forthcoming, they tend to become easily depressed

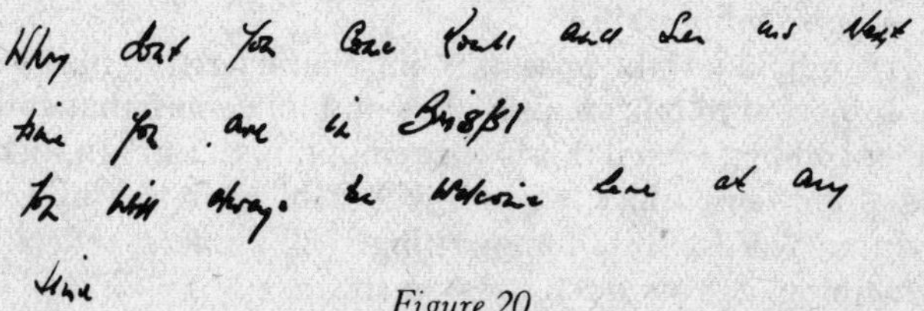

Figure 20.

Should each line of script ascend despite the overall constant appearance of the base line, it indicates an optimistic nature. These writers abound with enthusiasm and confidence although they sometimes lack sustained physical stamina.

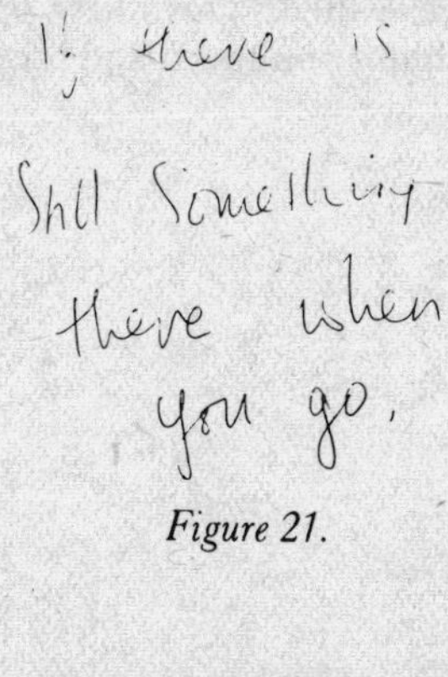

Figure 21.

Legibility

Once the overall appearance of the handwriting sample has been assessed the next thing to consider is whether or not the script is legible: is it easily readable or not?

Basically, it is fair to assume that someone who wishes to be understood, thinks clearly and is reasonably sincere will execute his script in a legible manner. However, there are positive and negative factors to all handwriting characteristics, therefore it is not safe to make the converse assumption. Good, clear writing does not always refer to good character, nor does poor legibility necessarily imply poor personality traits.

An individual who possesses fine characteristics may well be subjected to outside pressures and influences that cause inner conflict, even if this is of a temporary nature. In such a situation, these inner tensions will manifest in the subject's written words: his handwriting will suffer, reflecting something of this hidden stress or strain.

Legibility is not necessarily connected with the intelligence of the writer either. Often people worry needlessly about the impression their handwriting makes on others, feeling that others will consider them to be unintelligent or uneducated whereas, quite frequently, the real cause of the problem is the speed with which the writing has been executed. This latter point is dealt with more fully in the chapter on speed and pressure.

CHAPTER TWO

SIZE, SHAPE AND CONNECTIONS

Much can be deduced about a writer's self-esteem and, to a lesser extent, his creative abilities, by the overall size and shape of his handwriting and the manner in which he joins his letters together or, to use the graphological term, the connections.

Size

Generally speaking, the 'middle zone' letters of an average writing are about 3mm ($\frac{1}{8}''$). Middle zone letters are those such as the *n, m, o, e*, etc; in other words, letters that do not have upward or downward loops. So, middle zone letters larger than 3mm would be considered as large writing, and those of less than this would be termed small.

Basically, large writing refers to expansiveness. People with large handwriting (*Figure 22*) usually have a great

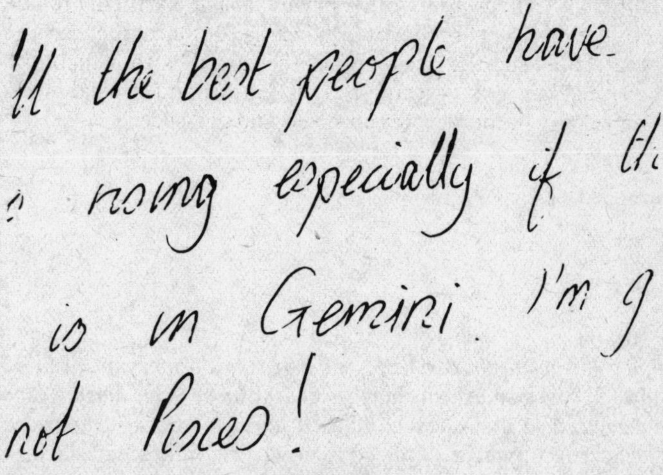

Figure 22.

desire for personal freedom and very much resent any sort of restriction. They take a broad outlook on life in general and their ambitions tend to be large-scale, in keeping with their expansive personalities. However, these open, self-confident folk are usually uninterested in finely detailed work and quickly become bored with it.

Small writing refers to creativity and a sense of detail. These writers are socially adaptable and tend to fit in easily in most environments. They tend to be slightly reserved and modest by nature and do not usually actively seek approbation or possess overriding ambition. Indeed, such individuals quite often lack self-confidence and can sometimes be a little too willing to fit in with the ways or schemes of others.

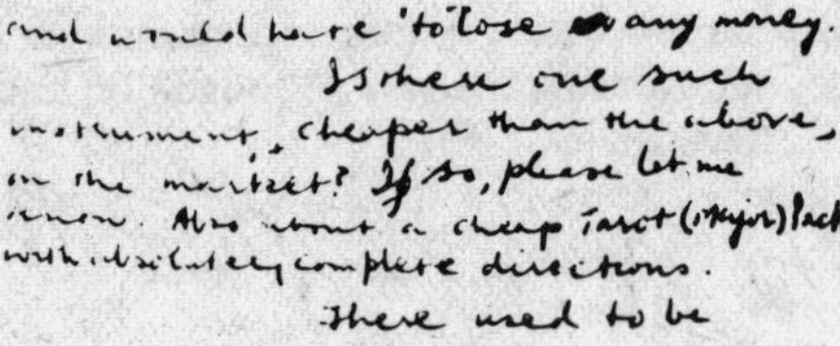
and would have 'to lose any money.
Is there one such
instrument, cheaper than the above,
on the market? If so, please let me
know. Also about a cheap Tarot (Major) pack
with absolutely complete directions.
There used to be

Figure 23.

Shape

Sometimes a handwriting has an overall appearance not so much of size as of height or tallness. The letters are executed in a slightly elongated manner and appear to be reaching upwards. This style of writing indicates a lack of objectivity and of consideration for others. Such writers may give the impression of smugness, or self-satisfaction at the expense of others.

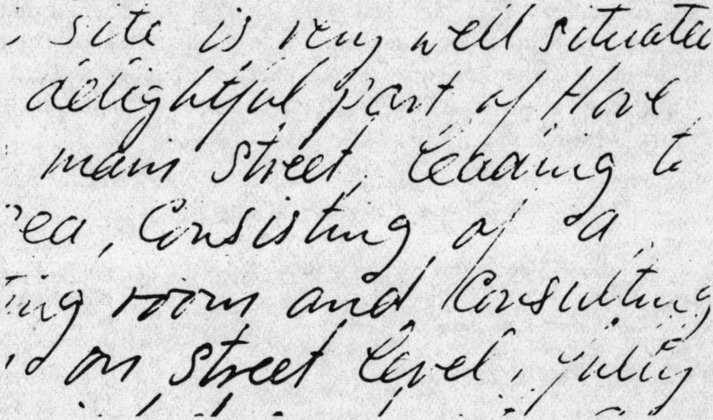

Figure 24.

The width of the handwriting indicates how much living space a writer wants for himself; and a broad or wide writing implies a boastful nature. These individuals possess egotism, pride and frankness – often to the point of bluntness; nevertheless, they usually present a friendly image to others and often display a strong desire to travel.

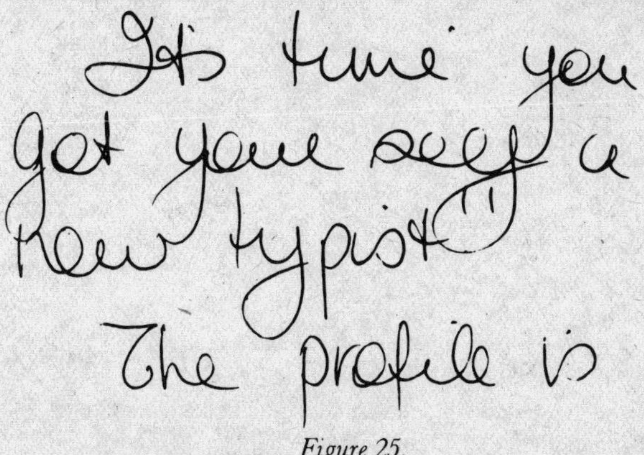

Figure 25.

Narrow writing implies inhibition, conservation and economy. Such writers are usually shy and exercise strong self-discipline; they are reluctant to disclose their inner natures to others because they are mistrustful of their motives. If the writing is so narrow that it appears 'squeezed', these traits become exaggerated to the extent of narrow-mindedness.

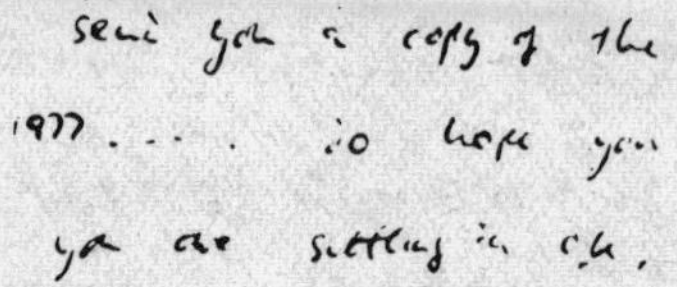

Figure 26.

Appearance
Thin writing – that is, one which has an overall 'spidery' appearance – indicates puritanism and a lack of sensuality. These individuals are mainly unconcerned or uninterested in the more material or earthy aspects of life. They concentrate their efforts on intellectual or spiritual pursuits, stressing the development of the more aesthetic side of their natures.

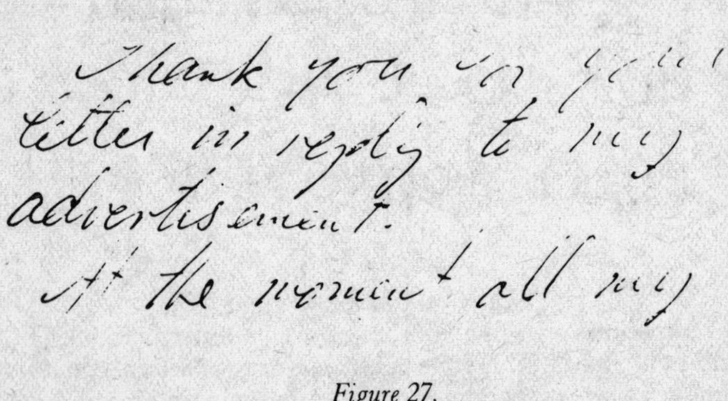

Figure 27.

Thick, heavy-lined writing – often referred to as 'pasty' by graphologists – is indicative of self-indulgence. These people enjoy the good things of life and actively indulge the more material aspects of their personality. If taken to extremes, this attitude can result in greed, selfishness, sensuality and arrogance, often combined with a lack of artistic taste.

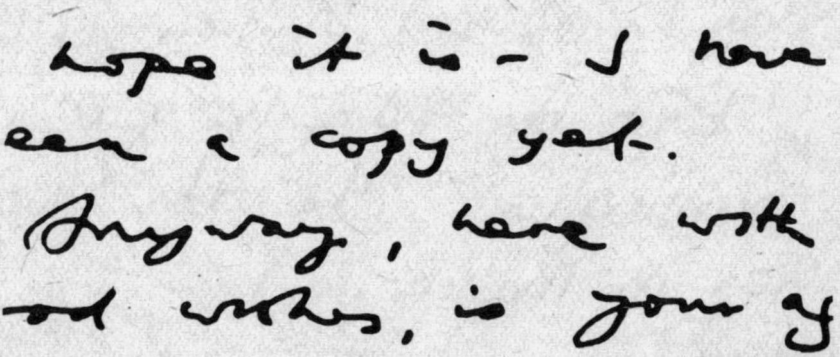

Figure 28.

Angular writing shows a certain hardness in the personality of the writer. Although they may be idealistic and imaginative, these folk tend to exhibit a slightly aggressive attitude to others. They often lack the ability or inclination to adapt their strongly-held views, sometimes to the point where stubbornness develops into downright prejudice.

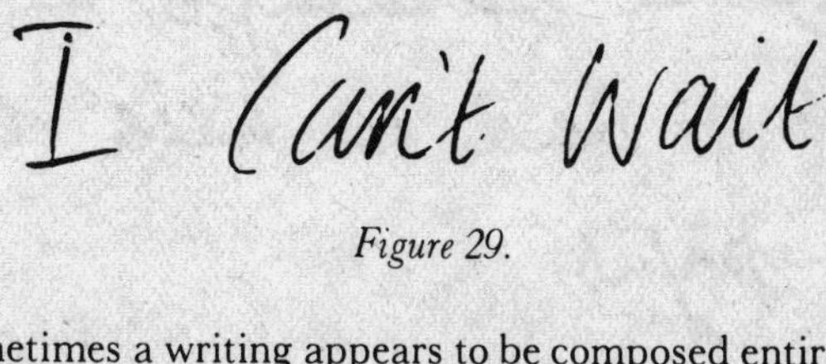

Figure 29.

Sometimes a writing appears to be composed entirely of a series of arches. This style of script is known as arcade and implies a lack of spontaneity. Noted for their diplomacy and good planning, such writers place a lot of importance on the impression they create on others. They tend to hide their inner thoughts and feelings and may, therefore, lack sincerity.

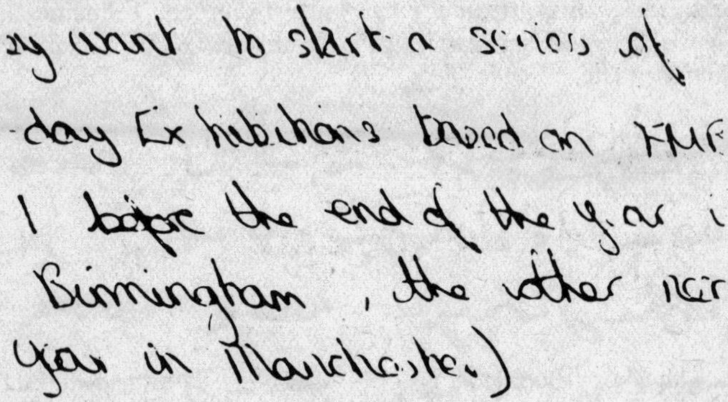

Figure 30.

Opposed to the arcade is the garland form of writing, which appears as a row of inverted arches. These individuals possess quiet, kind, sympathetic natures and present an easy-going, friendly, slightly extrovert image to others. Basically peace-loving, these people are easily imposed upon by others who tend to take advantage of their obviously good natures.

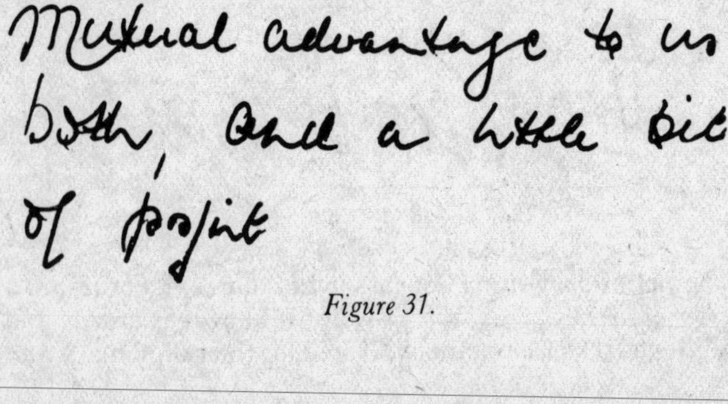

Figure 31.

A square look to the writing shows a concentration of effort and such writers often have an aptitude for mechanical or technical undertakings. They display sensible, down-to-earth attitudes, need firm foundations on which to build up their ideals, and are usually careful to take all aspects of a matter into consideration before announcing an opinion or delivering judgement.

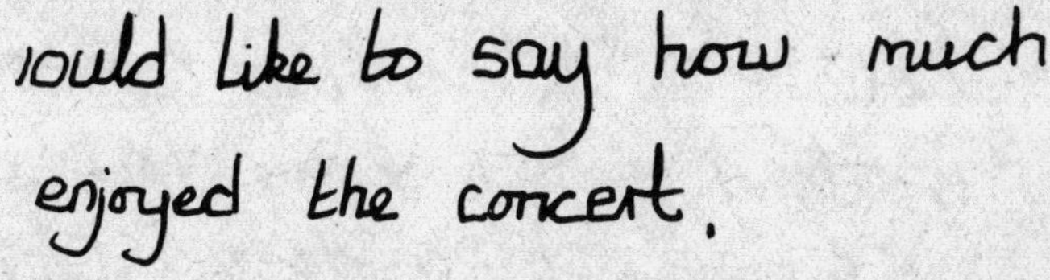

would like to say how much enjoyed the concert.

Figure 32.

The 'copy-book' formation – a simple, unadorned writing style – is indicative of orthodoxy and convention. These people are not strongly imaginative, tend to be rather conservative, but adapt well to almost any circumstances or environment. Lacking drive and ambition, these somewhat unexciting but reliable personalities are often the mainstay of their office or factory.

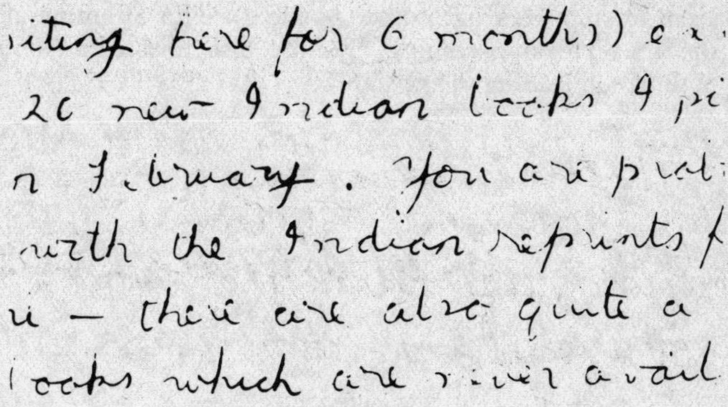

Figure 33.

Connections

A handwriting with a nice even appearance, each letter well constructed and connected, indicates a well-adjusted personality. People who execute this type of script are usually calm, considerate, exercise self-discipline and restraint. However, their lives tend to be rather monotonous and unexciting, and may appear dull and boring to others.

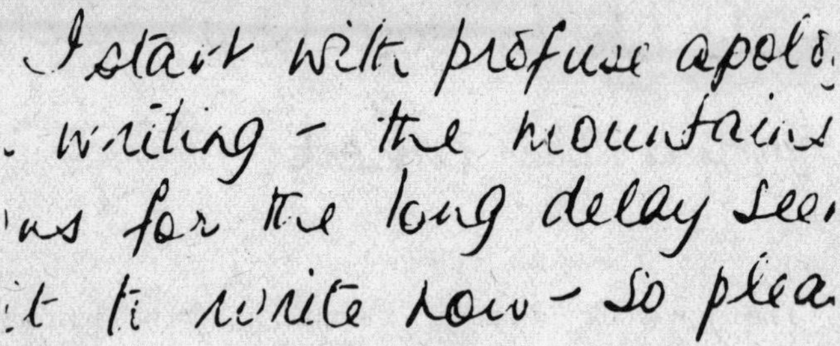

Figure 34.

Disconnected writing implies quite the reverse characteristics. These people lack control and are very easily distracted, particularly from routine tasks which do not retain their interest for long. Their imaginations never seem to stop working: numerous ideas vie for attention all the time. This may result in a jumpy, disconnected method of thinking, leading to unreliability.

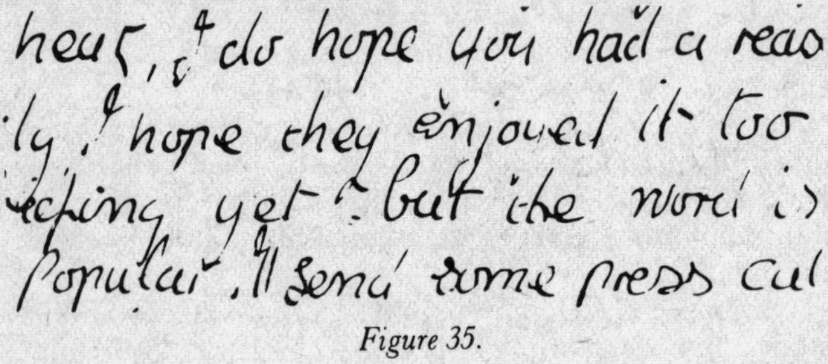

Figure 35.

A totally different, but easily recognizable form of connection is the thready type. These writers are extremely adaptable and possess great mental affinity. They have strong feelings of self-preservation and are highly capable of looking after their own interests, displaying an almost animal sense of cunning should it prove necessary to take evasive action.

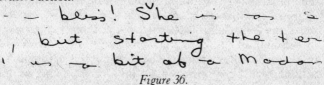

Figure 36.

General Observations

Basically, a handwriting will give an overall impression of roundness or angularity, and will furnish a clue to the overriding attitude of the writer.

The more rounded the writing, the greater the writer's inclination to be warm and affectionate. A passive, receptive nature will be the dominant characteristic of this personality although, in some cases, a more spontaneous demonstration of affection may be displayed. Conversely, the more angular or square the appearance of the script, the more unco-operative and critical the subject's basic nature is likely to be.

Very often one particular aspect of a handwriting changes considerably towards the end of the sample and this is indicative of the writer's attempts to hide his true character.

For example, the writing may start large and gradually diminish in size, or vice versa. This is often particularly noticeable in a handwritten application for a job, especially if the applicant feels at all doubtful of his abilities to obtain the post.

Obviously, therefore, it is of the utmost importance to study any handwriting specimen extremely carefully: consider all the aspects revealed, weigh them carefully, and never jump to conclusions – you could be misled.

CHAPTER THREE

DIRECTION: SLANT OF WRITING

The angle, or slant of a handwriting is an outward expression of the writer's emotional approach and response to others. It will illustrate whether the subject is basically impersonal and reserved; demonstrative and affectionate; or aloof and self-contained. The extent of this predominant attitude will be determined by the degree of the writing slope.

Forward sloping writing denotes the affectionate and gregarious types; those who are fundamentally extroverts by nature. Human relationships mean a great deal to these individuals who will usually choose vocations or occupations that will bring them into contact with others.

Those whose writing is basically upright or vertical are more reserved and self-contained; their heads tend to rule their hearts. These people are socially poised, polite and charming, but are inclined not to give too much of themselves in relationships. Realists, they choose their friends carefully.

A slant to the left indicates repressed tendencies. Such writers are not natural mixers and, being somewhat inhibited, often create an impression of cool detachment. Yet, once their trust has been gained, these people make dependable, loyal, long-lasting friends.

Sometimes an individual will exhibit two distinct styles of writing; perhaps writing with a natural forward slope most of the time but affecting an upright style on occasion. This reveals versatility. The writer's prevailing emotion at the time of writing will dictate the style, which will vary according to mood and circumstances.

Whereas the direction of writing slope will indicate the writer's basic personality traits, the degree or angle of slant will reflect the degree of emotional response at the time of writing. This overall angle of writing slant may be assessed from the illustration in Figure 37.

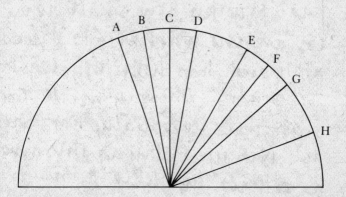

A   Selective and particular
B   Difficulty in adapting
C   Strong self-control
D   Slight reserve
E   Normal control
F   Less logical, more emotional
G   Impulsiveness
H   Poor self-control, extreme sensitivity

Figure 37.

Vertical Writing

Independence, cool judgement and stability are the characteristics revealed by a handwriting that is executed in a consistently upright or vertical manner. However, it is rare to find a perfectly upright writing. An allowance of about five degrees to either side of the vertical would, therefore, be classified as upright for the purposes of graphological analysis.

Although they may be emotionally intense, such writers are well able to contain their impulses and present a fundamentally matter of fact image to others. Eminently self-controlled, these people can be relied upon to keep their heads in a crisis (*Figure 38*).

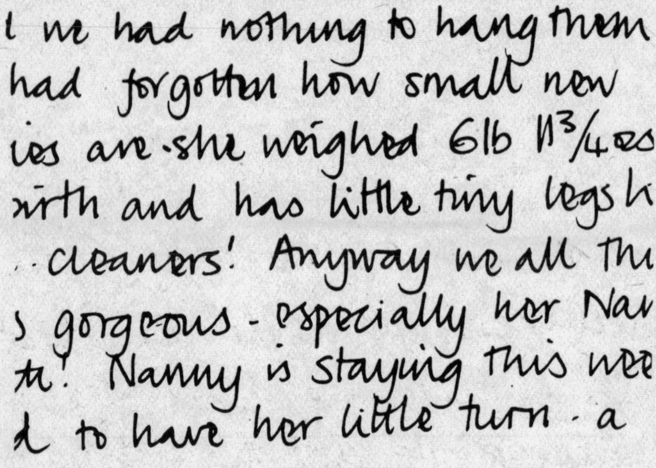

*l ne had nothing to hang them
had forgotten how small new
ies are · she weighed 6lb 11³/₄ es
birth and has little tiny legs k
..cleaners! Anyway we all th
s gorgeous · especially her Nan
th! Nanny is staying this wee
d to have her little turn · a*

Figure 38.

This controlled, intellectual approach leads these individuals to make good supervisors, managers and the like. For, although such people can work successfully as part of a team, they much prefer to work on their own because they value their independence. Therefore, these personalities are temperamentally suited to positions of responsibility which enable them to utilize these abilities to best advantage.

As stated earlier, a perfectly vertical handwriting is unusual and even a minimal inclination to left or right will disclose slightly differing characteristics. A writing that

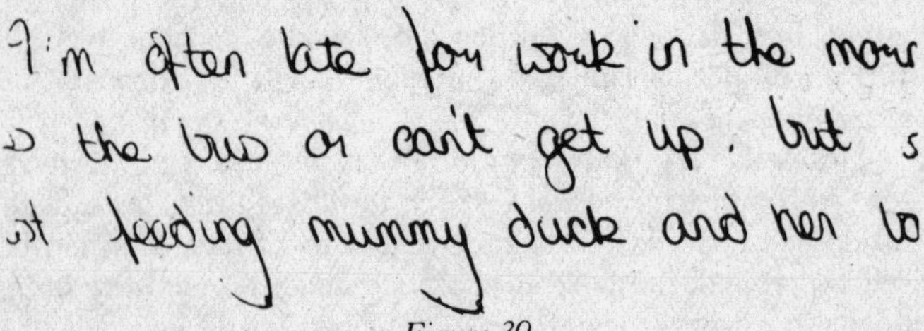

*I'm often late for work in the morn
o the bus or can't get up. but s
st feeding mummy duck and her to*

Figure 39.

slopes a little to the right, for example, (*Figure 40*) indicates slightly more out-going tendencies than the more reserved, leftward slant (*Figure 39*).

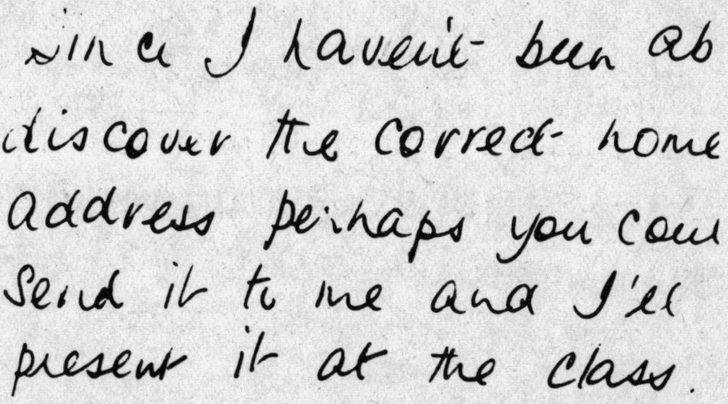

*since I haven't been ab
discover the correct home
address perhaps you cou
send it to me and I'll
present it at the class.*

Figure 40.

Similarly, the pressure with which a vertical writing is executed can give additional information about the writer. Although speed and pressure are dealt with more fully elsewhere, it is perhaps worth noting that heavy pressure in a predominantly upright writing denotes a slightly more emotional personality.

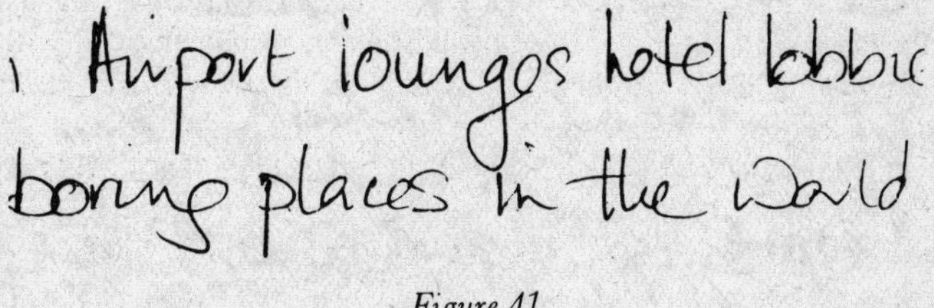

*Airport lounges hotel babbu
boring places in the world*

Figure 41.

Light-pressured writing refers to inner conflicts and, often, such a writer may have a little less control over his emotional responses. Such folk may, when the strain becomes too great, display short, sharp outbursts of temper – sometimes surprising themselves and others.

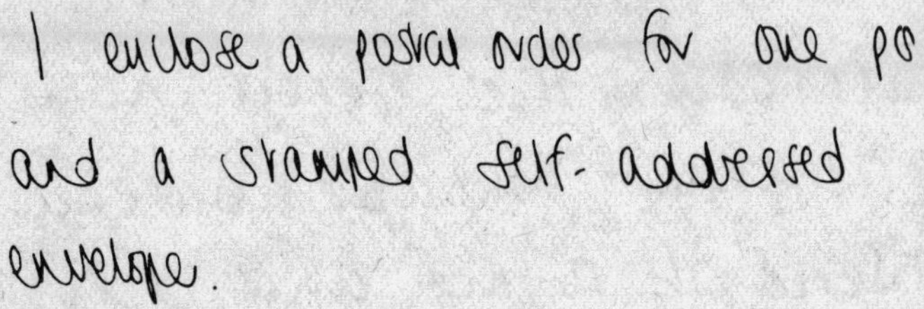

I enclose a postal order for one po and a stamped self-addressed envelope.

Figure 42.

Right-hand Slant

A consistently forward or right-hand sloping writing is very usual; indeed, it is probably the most natural angle for a right-handed person to use. This slant denotes a more extroverted personality than does upright writing, and the more acute the angle the more intensely emotional and responsive the writer is likely to be.

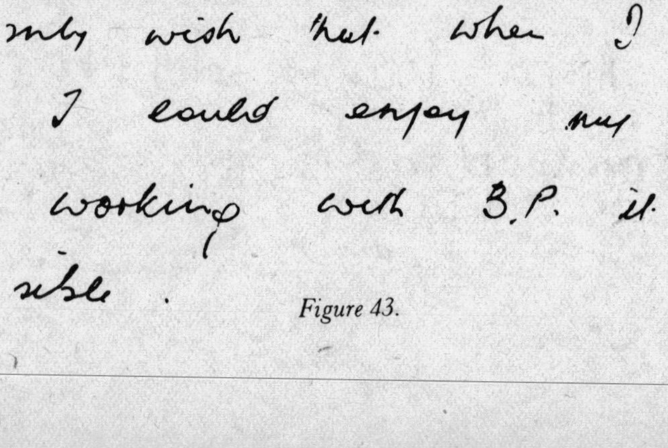

only wish that when I I could enjoy my working with B.P. it ible.

Figure 43.

Writing with a right-hand slope of about 60° denotes a warm, friendly, responsive personality. These individuals are reasonably self-confident and able to express their opinions and convictions in a natural, acceptable manner. Their self-control is average and, although they can be quite enthusiastic, these folk do not usually over-react or display excessive emotionalism.

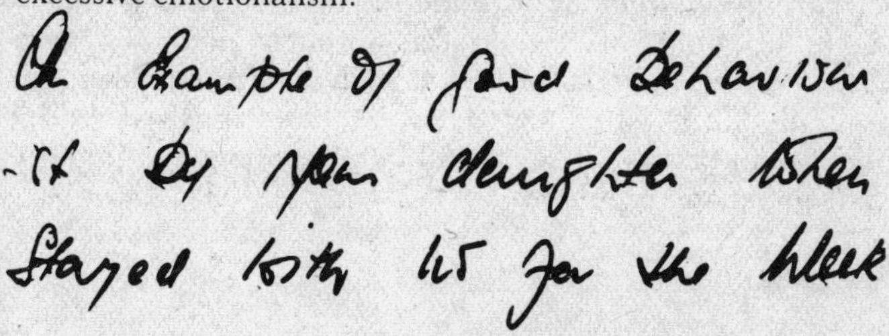

Figure 44.

When the forward slope is executed at an angle less than 60° from the horizontal it indicates a less well-controlled, more impulsive character. Such writers tend to rely on others for stimulation and actively seek the company of their fellows.

Indeed, human relationships play a major part in the lives of these restless, active, sociable individuals who tend to worry unduly about future events and their ability to cope with them. Yet they possess a reasonable degree of initiative and, as long as they work in convivial surroundings, are able to express their full potential.

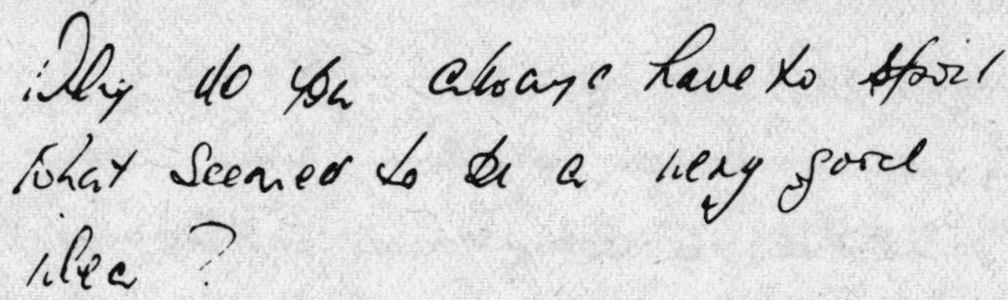

Figure 45.

An extreme right-hand slant – one of less than 45° – implies a lack of self-control and over-active responsiveness. Intense and often over-sensitive, these personalities tend to behave in an impulsive, rather irrational manner, sometimes creating a false impression of supreme confidence.

Not always reliable in some respects, such folk tend to lack the ability to see projects through and often drop schemes and interests almost as soon as they are taken up. Usually quick-witted and active, they are quickly bored by details and are most successful in occupations that require an immediate response.

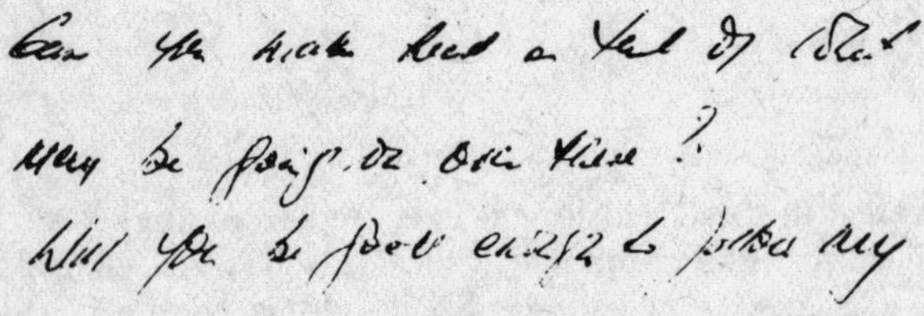

Figure 46.

Left-hand Slant

A backward or left-hand sloping writing is indicative of the introvert. It denotes a tendency for the subject to hold back, to hide his true inner feelings and opinions from the world at large. Such writers build up a protective shell around them and present an aura of self-containment and lack of emotional response to outsiders.

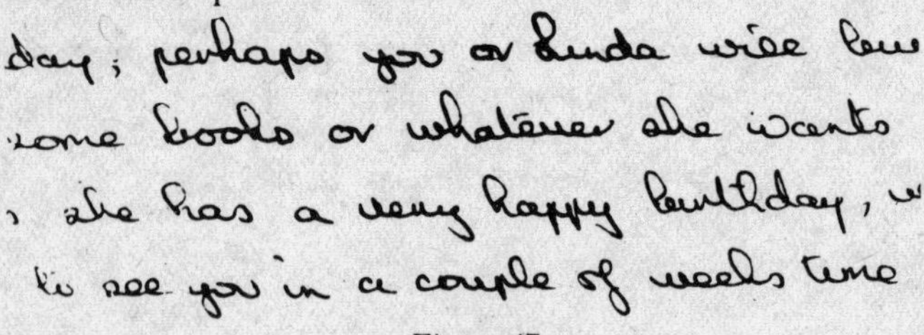

Figure 47.

These individuals are very restrained and careful not to exhibit their emotions, unless they know another extremely well, because they are ever conscious of their own vulnerability.

Self-controlled, these individuals are somewhat inhibited and tend to fear outward displays of emotion, whether their own or those of others. They are, therefore, not usually impulsive although, on rare occasions, the mask will slip and the onlooker will probably be greatly surprised at the depth of feelings thus revealed.

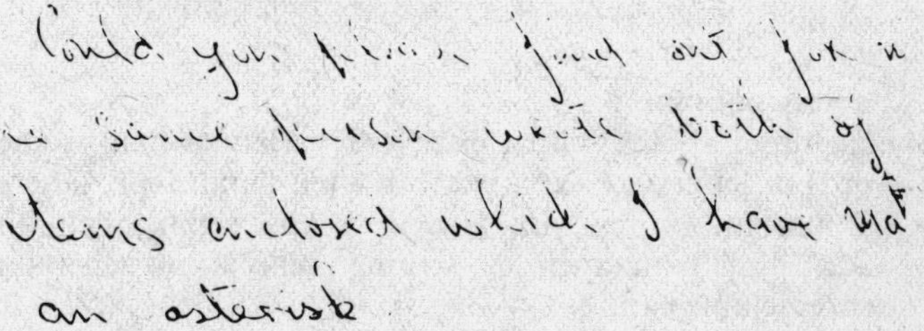

Figure 48.

The more a backward sloping writing is angled to the left the more these traits are accentuated. Such writers are likely to be too restrained and experience increasing difficulty in expressing themselves physically. These individuals are often objective and may not find it easy to adapt to new people, circumstances or environments.

They have a tendency to be over particular in their choice of friends owing to their inhibitions and their overwhelming desire to hide their emotions. Although basically independent, and despite outwards appearances, these folk are often deeply emotional and very sensitive.

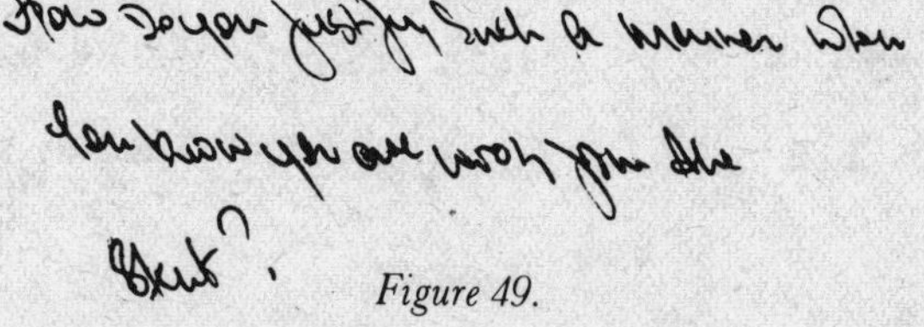

Figure 49.

An extreme left-hand slant emphasises the writer's repressive tendencies. These traits, when taken to extremes, can result in the subject attempting to evade reality and responsibility entirely.

Such writers sometimes appear cold and heartless, yet this apparent indifference may merely reflect the individual's desire not to become too emotionally involved. Often, early experiences have caused such personalities to become more withdrawn and, unfortunately, this apparent unsociability can result in real, rather than imagined isolation.

Variety of Slant

Sometimes a handwriting exhibits a variety of slant: some words or letters are executed with a left-hand slope, others are upright, a few are angled to the right. Such an undisciplined manner of writing reflects a generally unpredictable nature.

Versatile, spontaneous and temperamental, these writers are often so intense that they have difficulty in exercising any self-control. This lack of restraint arises from their fluctuating moods and the sheer depth of their emotions. Although they sometimes make efforts to control their moodiness and strong feelings, these subjects find it virtually impossible to persist in these efforts for long.

Their natures are too changeable, too subject to outside influences and the attractions of differing undertakings; they need variety in all they do. Their responses are quick and, usually, short-lived; but because of their underlying versatility, these subjects do well in occupations offering variety and requiring only limited responsibility (*Figure 50*).

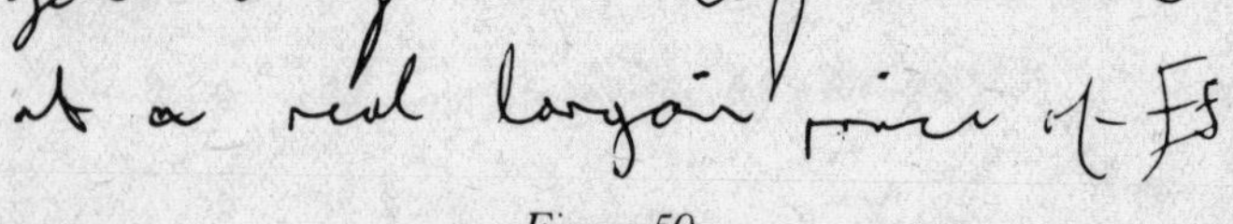

Figure 50.

CHAPTER FOUR

THE ZONES

Traditionally, handwriting is classified into three graphological zones or areas – upper, middle and lower – and every letter formation enters or occupies one or more of these zones. Each zone is attributed to one particular aspect of the personality, and the more that one particular zone is emphasized the more that particular set of associated characteristics will predominate. This is especially the case when a letter enters a zone with which it is not normally associated.

Figure 51.

The upper zone refers to inspiration, ambition,

intellectual or spiritual matters. The letters principally
involved are the *b, d, f, h, k, l* and *t*; all of which normally
enter the upper area. Strictly, the lower case *i* falls in this
section because of its dot, but a fuller interpretation of its
indications has been included in the chapter dealing with
this and other special letters (pp.70-2).

Middle zone letters – those without ascenders and
descenders – are *a, c, e, m, n, o, r, s, u, v, w* and *x*. These
letters, which are normally formulated without ascending
or descending loops, denote the writer's reactions and
attitude to mundane day-to-day matters, relationships,
environment and his general behavioural patterns.

The lower zone signifies the subject's more instinctual
desires: sexual and biological drive, sports interests,
possessiveness and materialism. The letters *g, j, p, q, y* and *z*
fall into this category. Also, although included in the upper
zone letters, the letter *f* enters the lower zone too and is,
therefore, referred to in this context.

The Upper Zone

Upper zone letters will indicate the extent to which a writer
pursues his ambitions, dreams and ideals. They show how
much he speculates, whether or not he has a vivid
imagination, how idealistic or ambitious are his aims.

A script that emphasises this upper sphere, to the
detriment of the middle and lower zones, implies that the
subject may lack practicality in his overall approach and
attitude to life.

When the upper zone loops – the ascenders – are
executed in a more or less conventional manner (*Figure 52*)

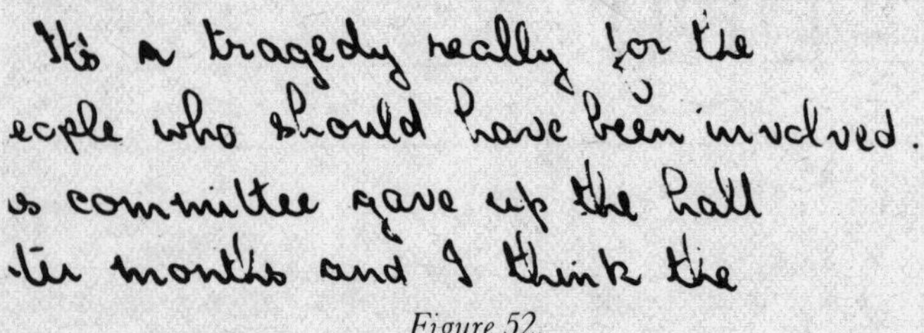

Figure 52.

it indicates that the writer's desires, aims and ambitions, hopes and wishes are the average ones. There is no particular emphasis placed on the more ideological side of his nature; his ambitions and ideals conform to the accepted norm; his general outlook is sensible and balanced. Such a writer is, in fact, a realist.

If these upper loops are stressed more than the middle zone letters, however, it implies that the personality is almost entirely concerned with intellectual pursuits. These folk are the idealists, the dreamers; they lack practicality and sometimes become so out of touch with reality that they are vain, proud and over-sensitive to criticism. Yet these are also the creative, imaginative individuals; the visionaries who can inspire others with their dreams and ambitions.

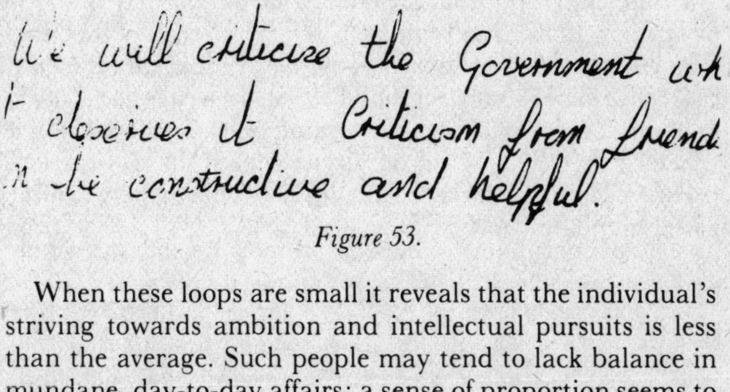

We will criticise the Government wh it deserves it Criticism from friend n be constructive and helpful.

Figure 53.

When these loops are small it reveals that the individual's striving towards ambition and intellectual pursuits is less than the average. Such people may tend to lack balance in mundane, day-to-day affairs; a sense of proportion seems to be absent from their characters. Although these writers may have good ideas and be mentally alert, they are sometimes unable to apply their ideals practically because of an inattention to detail.

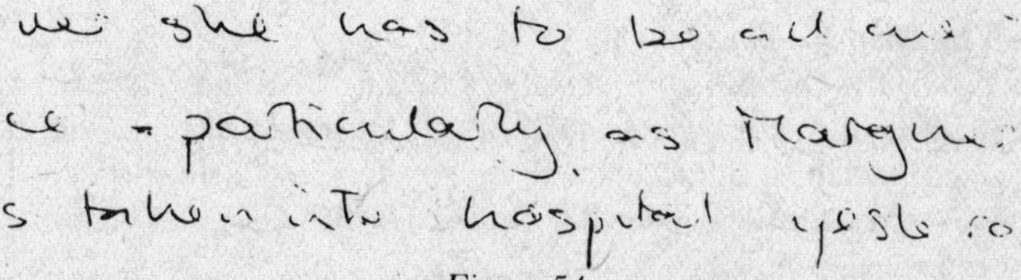

*we she has to be all as
e particularly as Margue
s taken into hospital yesta*

Figure 54.

Sometimes one sees a handwriting sample where the ascenders are so small that they are virtually non-existent. Such a formation is indicative of a personality who is so cautious in his mental approach that he is reluctant to allow his imagination any freedom of expression at all. He will tend to concentrate his efforts in more everyday affairs, lacking the ability to put his ideas across to others.

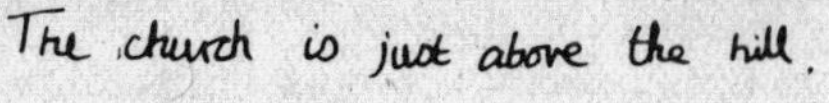

The church is just above the hill.

Figure 55.

Upper extensions that are comprised of very narrow loops or straight lines usually refer to a lack of creative thought. These individuals are not imaginative or idealistic; they are basically logical and methodical. Such writers are often good planners, capable of working out the details of a scheme so that it can be implemented in a practical manner. Rational and realistic, these people usually exhibit good, sound judgement.

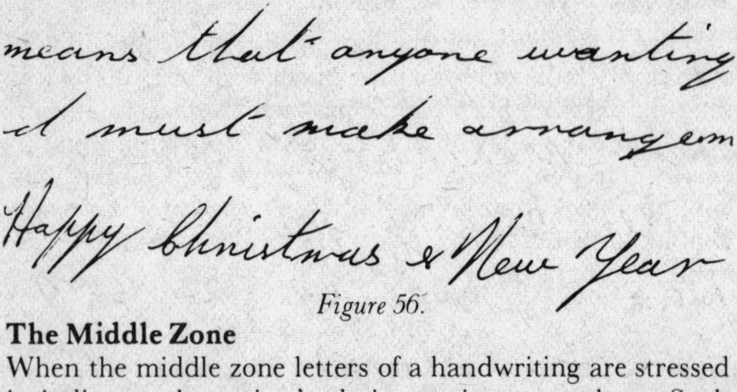

means that anyone wanting

d must make arrangem

Happy Christmas & New Year

Figure 56.

The Middle Zone
When the middle zone letters of a handwriting are stressed it indicates the writer's desire to impress others. Such people wish to be noticed, to be the centre of attention, and will sometimes become domineering in order to achieve their desired ends.

These traits are particularly emphasized when the middle zone writing dominates the other two zones. These people tend to live for the present; they are sociable and enjoy the company – and attention – of others. Yet these folk are not overly materialistic; they are basically unconcerned with making or retaining money and are more interested in impressing other people with the strength of their personalities than with their possessions.

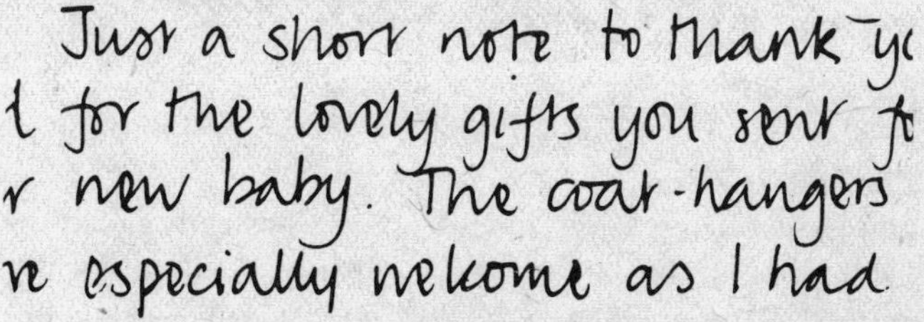

Just a short note to thank yo
l for the lovely gifts you sent f
r new baby. The coat-hangers
re especially welcome as I had

Figure 57.

When the middle zone dwarfs the lower zone letters it implies that the subject's personality is somewhat superficial. Such writers are not particularly influenced by the more instinctual side of their natures. Their self-expression is, however, well-marked and these folk are self-confident, capable and keenly ambitious in the purely practical sense. Socially, these individuals present a pleasant, likeable image and are good company.

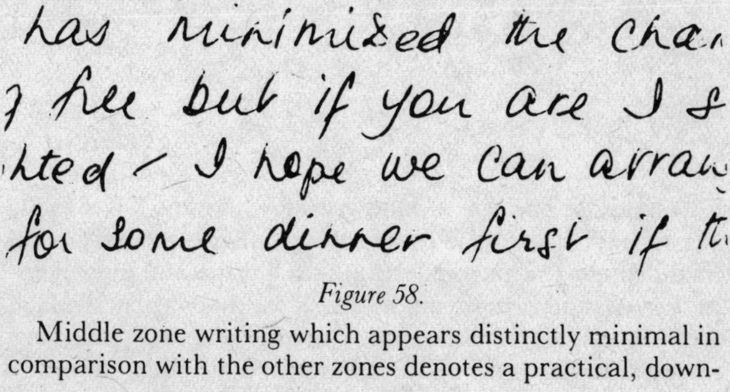

has minimised the chan
g hee but if you are I s
hted – I hope we can arran
for some dinner first if t

Figure 58.

Middle zone writing which appears distinctly minimal in comparison with the other zones denotes a practical, down-to-earth personality. These individuals possess abundant good sense, good physical stamina and, often, keen business abilities. However, they may well feel a certain dissatis-faction with their current career, social or sexual life and be actively seeking new fields to conquer; usually with successful results.

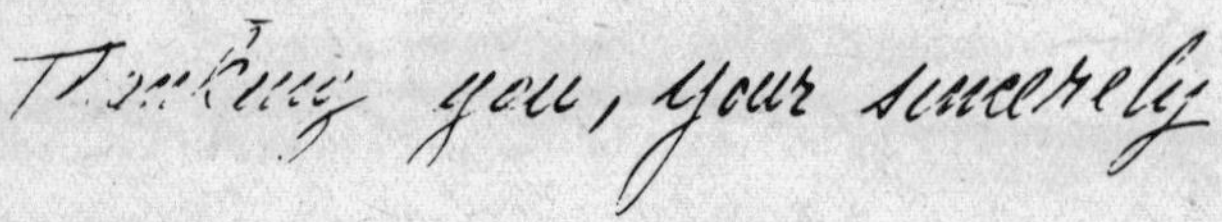

Thinking you, your sincerely

Figure 59.

The Lower Zone

Emphasis on the lower zone denotes a basically down-to-earth character. These folk often set much store by possessions or material achievements, but are quite prepared to work hard to achieve their ambitions. The fuller these lower loops the greater the writer's basic appetites are likely to be. Such individuals are predominantly interested in physical or outdoor activities; their sex drive is strong; and they tend to be rather materialistic.

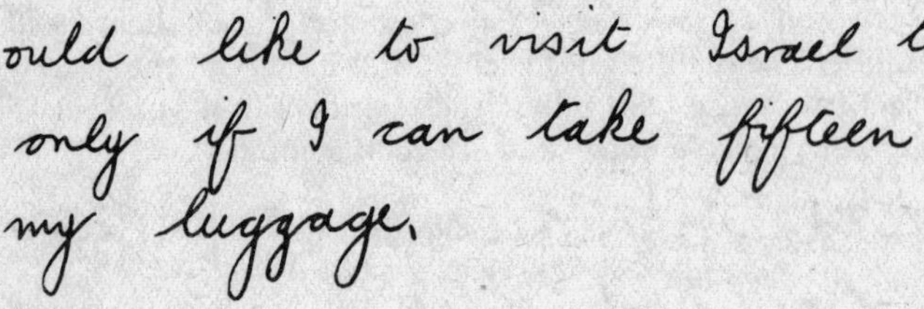

ould like to visit Israel to only if I can take fifteen my luggage.

Figure 60.

Sometimes one sees a handwriting where the lower loops are so long that they become entangled with the writing on the line below. This indicates a lack of order and judgement in the basic personality make-up. These people usually lack the ability to think logically or methodically and are inclined to be somewhat disorganised in their everyday lives, tending to muddle through. Often the sporty, outdoor types, these writers concentrate their efforts on the more physical pastimes.

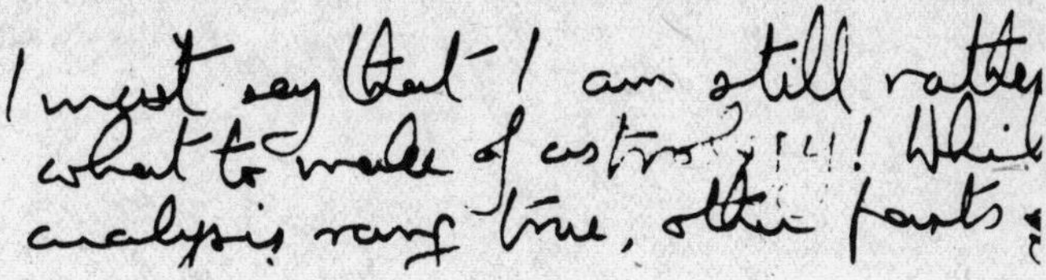

Figure 61.

A contentious attitude is revealed when the lower loops are formed with wide bases, particularly if these bases are rather angular in appearance. And, the further such loops reach, the greater the writer's tendency to exaggerate. Such individuals are impulsive, often rash, and rather self-opinionated. They tend to oppose anything new, usually without giving the matter any prior consideration: almost as a matter of principle.

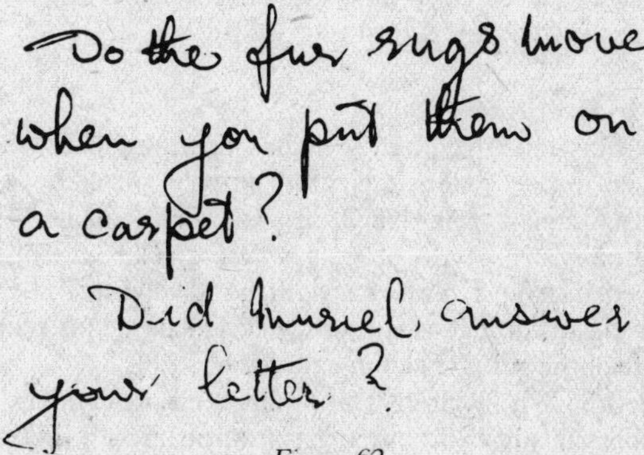

Figure 62.

Unusual lower loop formations often signify eccentricity, particularly in respect of sexual matters. Such loops may refer to sexual repression or unusual physical drive or desires. If these formations appear frequently in a handwritten sample it is allegedly indicative of an unusually passionate lover.

The first fifty pages

Figure 63.

A lack of loops or simple, straight lines to the lower zone reveals good judgement and an economy of expression. These moderate strokes denote the slightly moody, laconic character; but, often, such a person also has a marked musical or mathematical ability.

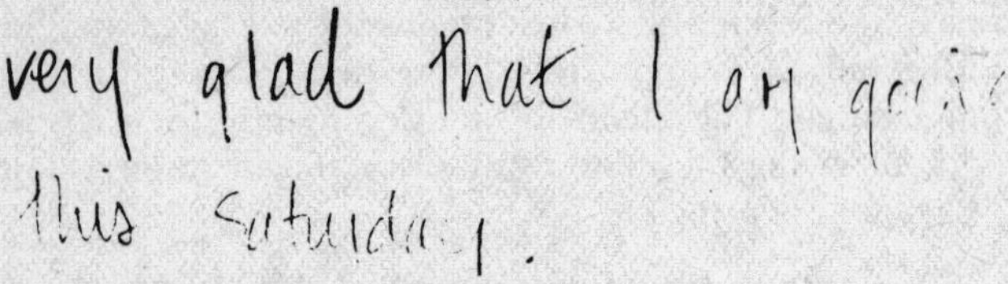

very glad that I am going this Saturday.

Figure 64.

Other Indications

Oddly, but not infrequently, it has been noted that lower loops or upper extensions that appear broken or not properly formed refer to a broken or deformed limb. Occasionally this type of incomplete stroke will only be produced during a temporary illness involving the loss of use of a limb; almost as if these writing extensions reflected the state of the subject's own extensions.

Sometimes a writer will make his ascenders and descenders in such a manner that it appears as if there were

to restore my confidence I get

Figure 65.

loops within loops. This rather ornate formation denotes dogged persistence – sometimes to the point of compulsion. These people will continue to pursue matters long after it ceases to be necessary; they are, in fact, natural worriers.

Figure 66.

In general terms, a loop may be described as an avenue of emotion and offers a clue to the way in which a writer will express his inner self to others. The wider a loop appears, for instance, the more expansive and outgoing the personality of the individual concerned. An entertainer, for example, often produces wide upper and lower loops, thereby expressing his sensitivity.

CHAPTER FIVE

CAPITAL LETTERS

Capital letters can be very revealing pointers in the analysis of personality traits. These upper case characters signify the basic strength and nature of the individual's ego. Whether plain and simple, elaborate and ornate, large or small in relation to the rest of the script, they will provide a guide to the writer's self-confidence and attitude towards authority.

Size
In general terms, the larger the capital the greater the individual's self-esteem is likely to be. Conversely, small letters indicate modesty, even humility.

For example, a tall but narrow capital letter implies that although the subject exhibits a certain degree of shyness in his approach to others, he still possesses self-assurance. Such a formation, therefore, illustrates the duality of the writer's nature: his inner esteem and confidence and the image that he wishes to present to the outside world.

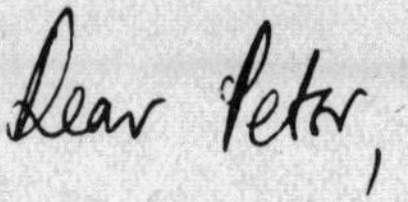

Dear Peter,

Figure 67.

A wide capital which dwarfs the rest of the writing reveals an expansive nature. These people are very confident and tend to impose their opinions on others. If this type of capital letter is also rather ornate, these traits will be emphasized. In such a case, the writer is likely to be somewhat conceited and 'pushy', perhaps to the point of vulgarity.

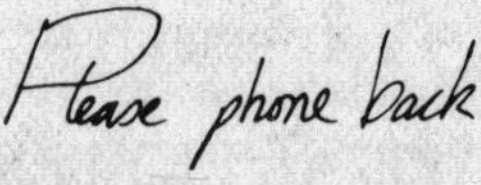

Please phone back

Figure 68.

Small or low-set capitals denote a basically modest, uncomplicated personality. Such people are usually conventional, reserved and slightly old-fashioned in their views. Naturally unassuming, these folk sometimes experience difficulty in expressing themselves; but any such lack of self-assertiveness will be verified by other indications in the handwriting.

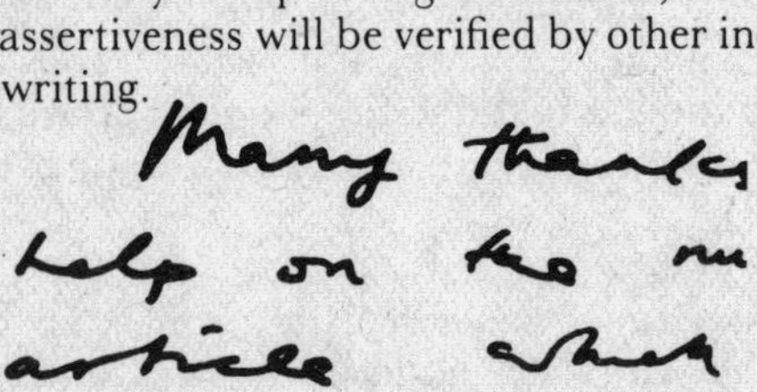

*Many thanks
help on the
article which*

Figure 69.

Tiny capitals – those that are the same size as the rest of the script or even smaller – indicate a very retiring, unpretentious, unobtrusive character. Usually, such small upper case letters are also formed in a very simple, unadorned manner, implying that the writer is lacking in self-confidence and tends to underestimate his own abilities and worth.

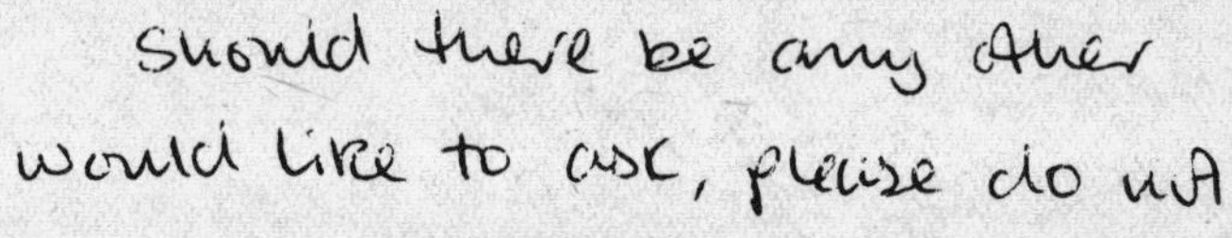

Should there be any other

would like to ask, please do not

Figure 70.

Ornamentation

Broadly, the more ornate the capital the more flamboyant the personality of the writer; the greater his need to assert his personality and impress others.

For instance, all capitals with an extra stroke coming in from the left indicate an added sense of importance in the writer's concept of the self. These strokes may be regarded as props for the writer, as are any forms of exaggeration to a letter. When such an additional flourish originates from the middle or lower zone, it signifies the individual's physical pride and vanity.

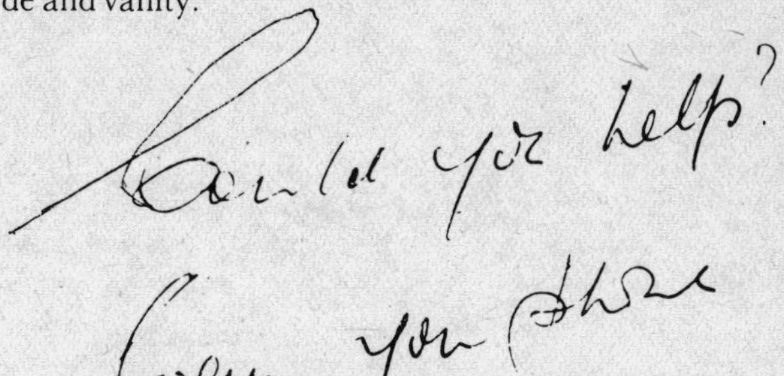

Could you help?

Can you show

Figure 71.

A capital that is ornamented with an extra stroke coming in from the upper zone denotes intellectual vanity. Such people are self-opinionated: they not only think they are superior to others, they 'know' that they are. Usually intractable, these individuals are seldom influenced by the ideas or ways of others because of their high regard for themselves and their abilities.

Figure 72.

An exaggerated loop to the left of a capital letter reveals selfishness and sensuality. When such a stroke is also very ornate these traits are emphasized, sometimes to the extent of greed, megalomania, egotism and, in some instances, homosexual tendencies. It should be remembered, however, that other indications in the script may negate or alleviate these extreme tendencies.

Figure 73.

Other Formations
Sometimes a writer will exaggerate the top of his capital letter in such a way that it will encircle the remainder of the word. This formation signifies self-dramatization, and a tendency to patronise others due to strong self-protective

instincts. Such writers may, therefore, exhibit a certain amount of insincerity and prove somewhat unreliable.

Figure 74.

The inverse formation of the one mentioned above – where the lower part of the capital letter is used to underline the rest of the word – emphasizes the vanity and self-approbation of the writer. Again, he is trying to direct the attention of others to the ego – the I — and this subconscious desire is reflected in the manner in which these capitals stress the words written.

Figure 75.

A capital letter that starts in the lower zone – well below the established line of writing – and rises clear into the upper zone indicates an aggressive and fussy nature. These folk are very confident and determined to establish their opinions and methods on others because of their innate sense that their ways are the right ones.

Figure 76.

Occasionally one encounters a script where a capital letter appears in the wrong place: in the middle of a sentence or even in the middle of a word. These misplaced letters indicate the writer's unsettled state at the time of writing – he is not thinking clearly – and usually refer to a temporary problem or emotional upset which is disturbing the subject's powers of concentration.

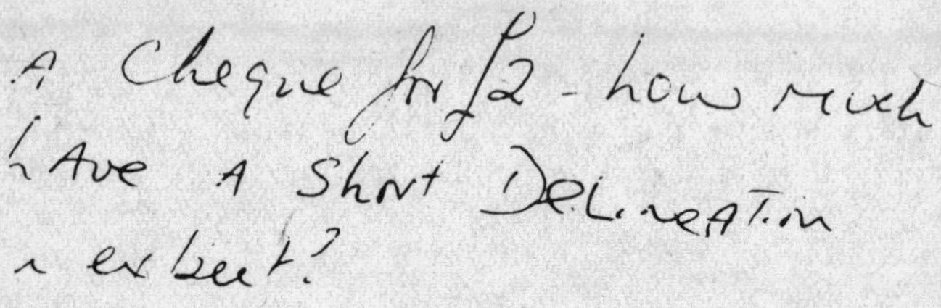

Figure 77.

CHAPTER SIX

PRESSURE AND SPEED: HEALTH AND MOOD INDICATORS

The main advantage of collecting samples of a person's handwriting over a period of time is that they will show variations of mood and fluctuations in the subject's well-being. If only one sample is available for analysis it will make the graphologist's task that much more difficult: certain possibilities will be evident, of course, but more positive assessments would not be practicable or wise.

However, periods of stress, carefree moments, physical health and emotional upheavals will all have some bearing on the manner in which an individual formulates his script. For example, the pressure and speed of a sample will furnish clues to the writer's health and mood at the time of writing.

Pressure

Graphologists measure a person's intensity of mood, vitality and determination by the amount of pressure he exerts in his handwriting. Yet few people realize just how heavily or lightly they move their pens across a page – it is almost always a purely subconscious action.

A fountain pen or a felt-tip will reveal the amount of pressure used by the way in which the strokes will spread out, sometimes creating a 'pasty' or blurred image. However, in these days of the ball-point pen, pressure is more often felt than seen.

Heavy pressure refers to a strong libido, endurance and resistance to exhaustion. Emotional strength and enthusiasm are other positive factors denoted by a heavy-pressured script, particularly if accompanied by speed of writing. Such a handwriting will, then, convey the impression of originating from a well-balanced, physically healthy, confident individual.

However, should such heavy pressure be observed in a slowly-executed script, it signifies that the writer's energies are poorly channelled and may indicate a depressed or frustrated personality. These traits are emphasized when such pressure appears intermittently throughout a handwriting sample.

Intermittent pressure refers to an inferiority complex and unsteady or uncontrolled will-power. Such erratic pressure often reflects a moody personality; someone whose inner conflicts and tensions combined with emotional instability result in feelings of insecurity and inconsistent responses.

Speed

Both speed and pressure are evident when the writer is following an idea through, whereas the writing will be executed at a slower rate as his thoughts slow down or when he encounters a difficult passage. This is an important factor to take into consideration, particularly when assessing the qualities of an applicant for a job.

Speed is, therefore, an indication of an alert mind, and slow-thinking folk rarely produce a fast script. Those who possess quick, sharp, penetrating minds write quickly and their spontaneous approach is usually indicated by a forward slanting script with the t-bars and i-dots well to the right.

Although the right-hand margin of a quickly executed script may be quite mixed, a left-hand margin that increases towards the bottom of the page is a good indication of speed. Another small pointer is the position of the full stops: as the speed of the writing increases so do these punctuation marks get further and further to the right – becoming detached from the rest of the sentence.

A slowly executed script – with carefully placed i-dots and lightish pressure – denotes an emotionally controlled personality. Such people are not usually inclined to moodiness and tend to present a consistent, though perhaps slightly reserved image to others, particularly if the writing is more or less vertical.

A slow and weak-pressured writing does not necessarily refer to poor health, but it may imply a delicate state of mind or body at the time of writing. This is especially so if there are obvious hesitations in the script, indicating that the writer is feeling slightly under par, either mentally or physically, at the time.

Basically, a handwriting that is executed at a constant pace denotes continuity of thought and adequate self-expression. These individuals are able to convey their ideas to others in a straightforward, confident manner and, if the script is evenly-pressured also, their self-assurance will be strong.

Health and Mood
Speed and pressure combined will, therefore, convey a person's physical and emotional state at the time of writing. And, apart from any minor indications of tiredness or

temporary ill-health, firm pressure and constant speed reflect a healthy and alert mind in a physically active body.

Physical ill-health is, however, often revealed in the angularity of a script. Such writing appears spiky and may also be faintly and hesitatingly executed. When a script is so untidy that it seems to go in all directions at once this is a pointer towards emotional tension or mental stress. Certain forms of disability are sometimes shown by broken loops in the upper or lower zone loops: a broken arm may be revealed by badly formed or broken upper zone loops; a broken or fractured lower limb may be reflected in poorly made or broken lower zone loops.

The mood of the moment may be revealed by the concave or convex appearance of the base line – an imaginary line along which the writing is placed. Although every effort may have been made to write in a nice straight line this is, in fact, an extremely difficult task. So, when such even writing does appear, it denotes strong determination and will-power. These individuals will control their emotions successfully through the application of reason and logic; they are likely to be even-tempered and reliable.

Conversely, a wavy appearance to the lines of script implies emotional imbalance. Such personalities are easily distracted and their writing frequently undulates despite the use of lined paper. Although these people may be rather more interesting than the more purposeful characters, they are less likely to be reliable and tend towards moodiness.

Very uneven lines of script coupled with unequal words and letters denotes unpredictability and noncomformity. Other factors in the script will indicate the degree of intensity of these traits but, basically, these are the type of people who are subject to extremes of mood. They are unreliable, often unconventional, and it may be impossible to keep track of their ideas, ambitions, actions and reactions.

CHAPTER SEVEN

REVEALING LETTERS

The study of handwriting can be a very complex affair and nowhere is this more vividly illustrated than by the numerous different formations of the letters *a, o, i* and *t*. Each variation of these four letters has been found to be linked to a specific characteristic and they are, therefore, deserving of a closer examination.

Obviously, each of us writes in a different style and every script is, therefore, quite individual. Nevertheless, a study of these particular letters will prove of great assistance in the analysis of an individual's personality traits. One should always bear in mind, however, that other indications in the script must be taken into consideration also for a complete interpretation to be made.

(1) THE LETTERS 'a' AND 'o'

The letters *a* and *o* are known as 'closed' letters and demonstrate the degree of openness in the personality, as do the middle zone sections of the letters *d* and *g*. At one time or other we all come into contact with people who can be considered to have open or closed natures and a study of these particular lower case letters will offer a clue to assessing which trait dominates.

Of course, there are occasions when we ourselves are more frank and communicative with our friends and colleagues than at others. Sometimes we exercise greater discretion and keep some information to ourselves; we become a little secretive and defensive. To what extent we exhibit these tendencies is revealed by the manner in which we form the letters *a* and *o*; and, to a lesser extent, the letters *d* and *g*.

Closed Formations

Closed tops to these letters denote a rather cautious personality. Such writers are not deceitful in any way, merely rather reserved in their general attitude. They have a tendency to keep their own counsel until they are quite sure of their ground and are not inclined to reveal personal details or discuss business matters with those they do not know well.

Figure 78.

Sometimes the final strokes of the *a* and *o* curve round to such an extent that they completely encircle these letters. This formation signifies an over-cautious nature, particularly on an intimate level. These individuals may communicate well on impersonal matters but, because of their inner feelings of insecurity, tend to withdraw from personal relationships or commitments.

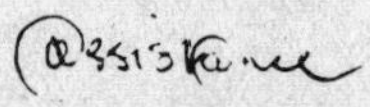

Figure 79.

A more extreme example of this enclosed formation is when the top part of the letters appear to be sealed with a little loop or knot. Such people are very self-contained and reserved; prefer to keep themselves to themselves; and tend to shy away from any friendly overtures. Their self-expression is usually somewhat limited and they may experience difficulty in responding to others.

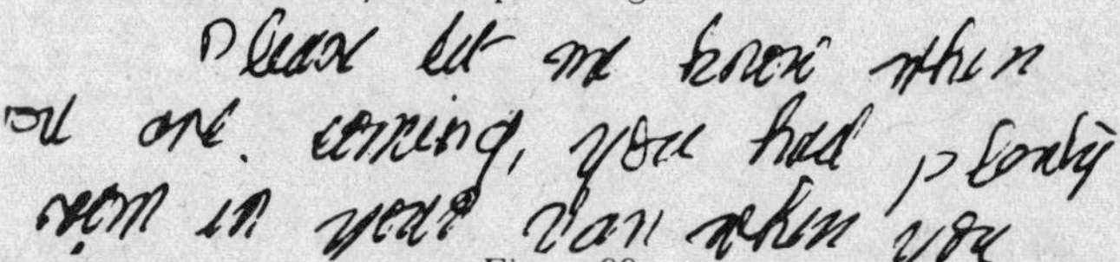

Figure 80.

Mixed Formation

It is quite common to find both open and closed formations in the same script and it is simply a question of exercising common sense when one is analysing a handwritten sample. Obviously, there are occasions when it pays dividends to be open and frank in one's dealings; equally, there are times when it is necessary to use a certain amount of discretion.

Discretion is clearly indicated by a script that includes both open and closed formations to these revealing letters. However, a careful study of the writing will be necessary to determine whether the subject is being frank or cautious at the right times and for the correct reasons.

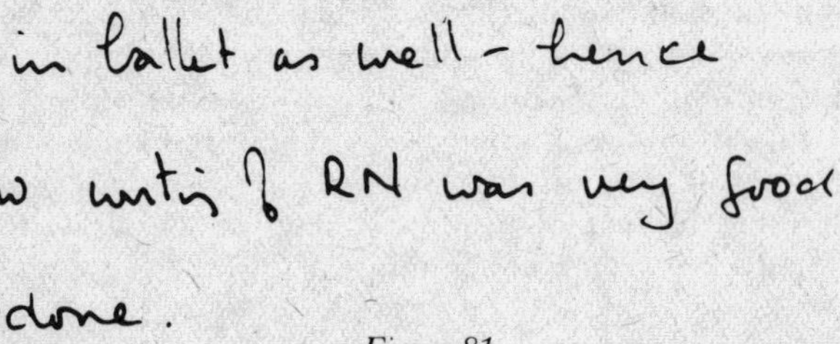

Figure 81.

Open Formations

A script where the top part of these letters is predominately open shows a generally frank and open personality. Such people are easy to get along with, they communicate well and are basically uncomplicated characters. Straight-forward and honest in their approach to others, these individuals make friends easily and fit into most environments due to their overt, friendly manner.

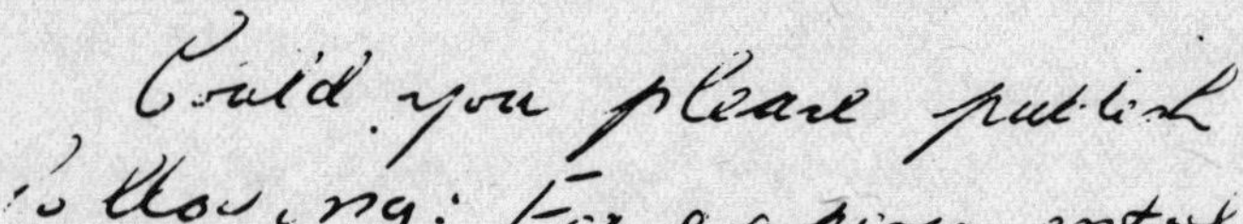

Figure 82.

Open formations at the base-line denote a slightly hypocritical nature. It might be considered unwise to trust such writers completely in all matters because they may well be trying to disguise their true motives by presenting a somewhat false image.

Figure 83.

Such untrustworthiness is accentuated if the *a* and *o* are formed with an opening to the left of the letter. Something of an egotist, this type of person will tend towards greed and selfishness; certainly he will put his needs before those of others and may prove unreliable as a result.

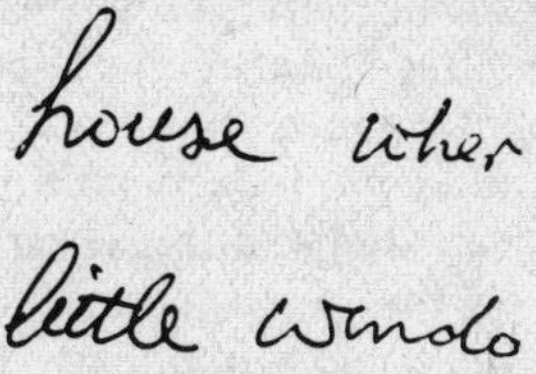

Figure 84.

When the middle zone sections of the *d* and *g* are left open, or if these letters appear to be written in two distinct parts, it signifies a degree of loquaciousness. If such an open formation to the letter *g* is combined with a long lower loop, this tendency will be accentuated to the point of garrulousness: these people are simply incapable of keeping anything to themselves! Equally talkative is the individual who makes an open *d* with a long upper loop; but he will probably have the ability to talk himself out of situations as well as into them.

Other Formations

Whether they are open or closed, when these revealing letters – the *a, o, d* and *g* – are very narrow it implies secrecy. Very occasionally one sees a script where these letters are formed so tightly that the circular configurations become filled in – almost appearing as blobs – and this indicates a basically sensual nature.

(2) THE LETTER 'I' AND 'i'

The letter *I* is commonly called the barometer of the ego. Eccentricity, pride, vanity, consideration, thoughtfulness, aggressiveness, reserve, shyness – all are traits that can be shown by the way in which this letter is executed. Indeed, so much can be detected from the various formations of the capital *I* that it is often referred to by graphologists as the 'private I'.

The capital *I* is the configuration that we look at for signs of the ego image: the projection of the self. Of course, its lower case counterpart can be equally revealing. Confidence, poise and assurance may be detected from the shape and dotting of this letter. Other traits to consider in addition to those already mentioned are precision, self-importance and mental scope.

Obviously, it would not be practicable to illustrate all the possible different formations of this letter as it reflects the individuality of the writer to such a high degree. However, the following are those most frequently encountered in a script and will provide some guidance to the student.

The Capital 'I' (Key to sample letters: Figure 85)

(a) Horizontal lines top and bottom – like a Roman numeral I: constructively clear thinking; usually willing; possible aptitude for mechanics or engineering.

(b) A simple, single, straight vertical stroke: maturity; conciseness; adherence to essentials.

(c) Upper loop more fully formed than the lower: intellectual self-importance.

(d) Lower loop more fully formed than the upper: physical self-importance.

(e) Retraced upper loop: timidity; dislike of talking about or drawing attention to self.

(f) Exaggerated size (irrespective of formation): inflated ego; self-opinionated.

(g) Small capital, same size as script: low opinion of the self.

(h) Arc to the left at base of letter: avoidance of responsibilities.

(i) Starting from the right: sense of humour; an open, friendly disposition.

The Lower Case 'i' (Key to sample letters: Figure 86)

(j) Precise dotting: precision; accuracy; restraint.

(k) Dot omitted: laziness; weakness or carelessness.

(l) Dot placed to left: caution; procrastination, introversion.

(m) Dot placed to right: enthusiasm; quick-thinking; extroversion.

(n) Semicircular dot to left: ultra-sensitivity; introspection.

(o) Semicircular dot to right: observant; perception.

(p) Circular dot: eccentricity; individualism; somewhat unrealistic; faddist.

(q) V-shaped dot: materialistic; sarcastic.

(r) Inverted v-shaped dot: strongly critical nature, both to self and others.

(s) Highly placed dot: imaginative; idealistic; unrealistic.

(t) Very low-placed dot: aptitude for highly detailed and precise work.

(u) Dot connected to letter on either side: clever; astute mentality.

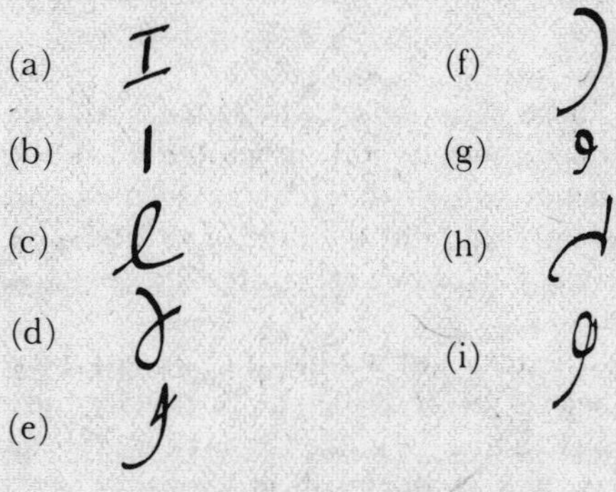

(a) $\mathcal{I}$ (f) $)$

(b) I (g) $\mathfrak{g}$

(c) ℓ (h) $\mathcal{d}$

(d) $\mathfrak{d}$ (i) $\mathfrak{g}$

(e) $\mathcal{f}$

Figure 85.

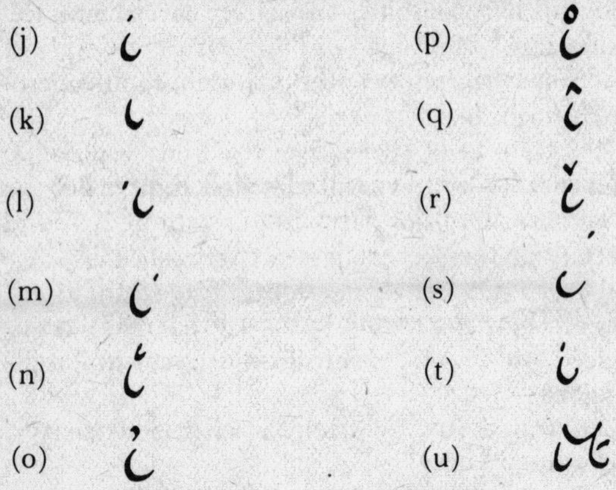

(j)	*ı*	(p)	*ℓ*
(k)	*ℓ*	(q)	*ℓ*
(l)	*'ℓ*	(r)	*ℓ*.
(m)	*ℓ'*	(s)	*ℓ*
(n)	*ℓ*	(t)	*ℓ*
(o)	*ℓ*	(u)	*ℓℇ*

Figure 86.

Slant of Letter

When the personal pronoun is used in capital form but slopes in the opposite direction to the rest of the script it implies a degree of selfishness or self-centredness in the nature. This is particularly emphasized when the *I* slopes to the right in a backward slanting script; indicating a 'me first' attitude at all times. However, when the *I* slopes to the left and the script to the right this self-centredness is more introspective; these subjects tend towards introversion and self-criticism.

(3) THE LETTER 'T'

There are probably more variations to the letter T and its lower case counterpart than to any other letter in the alphabet. The manner in which this letter is formed will indicate the emotional pressures at the time of writing, also the writer's strength of will-power, taste, health and ambitions.

The cross-bar of the letter *t* – rather like the *i* and its dot – is a free formation: there is no prescribed manner of forming it. For this reason, perhaps, it gives the writer a brief opportunity to express the self, albeit subconsciously.

The stem of this letter signifies the degree of idealism; the height of the cross-bar denotes the writer's level of ambition; and its length refers to the amount of self-control in the personality.

As with the letter *I*, there are too many possible variations of formation for them all to be listed here, but the following selection comprises the most commonly-found configurations.

The Capital 'T' (Key to sample letters: Figure 87)

(a) Long horizontal bar: patronising manner; self-protective instincts.

(b) Loop in cross-bar: tendency towards criticism; sensitivity; astuteness.

(c) Fussy or ornate formation: poor artistic taste.

(d) Left tending curve at base: tendency to live in the past to the detriment of the present.

The Lower Case 't' (Key to sample letters: Figure 88)

(e) Short cross-bar: lack of self-control; dislike of imposed disciplines.

(f) No cross-bar: absent-mindedness; preoccupation or carelessness.

(g) Bowed cross-bar: self-control; restraint; possibly somewhat inhibited.

(h) Hook on bar to the left: acquisitive nature; materialistic.

(i) Hook on bar to the right: tenacity; resolution.

(j) Ascending cross-bar: optimism; aggression; a degree of ambition.

(k) Descending cross-bar: determination; moodiness or sullenness.

(l) High cross-bar: bossiness; strongly ambitious.

(m) Bar arcs from base of stem: deceitful nature; an opportunist.

(n) Bar to the right: quick-thinking; astute mentally.

(o) Bar to the left: cautious nature; procrastination.

(p) Wavy bar: sense of humour; fun-loving personality.

(q) Simple 'x' formation: an eye for small details; tendency to let larger issues slide.

(r) Star formation: responsibility; reliability; common sense.

(s) Star with a loop: persistence; tenancity; materially possessive.

(t) Long cross-bar linking two letters or words: mental agility; good practical planning ability.

(u) Crossing back: jealousy; egotism; self-pity.

(v) Double or split stemmed: laziness, slow thinking or acting.

(w) Looped stem: loquaciousness; sensitivity; vanity, prejudice; nonconformist tendencies.

(x) Long stem: idealism; intellectually inclined.

(y) Short stem: timidity; conservative and conventional nature.

(a)

(b)

(c)

(d)

Figure 87.

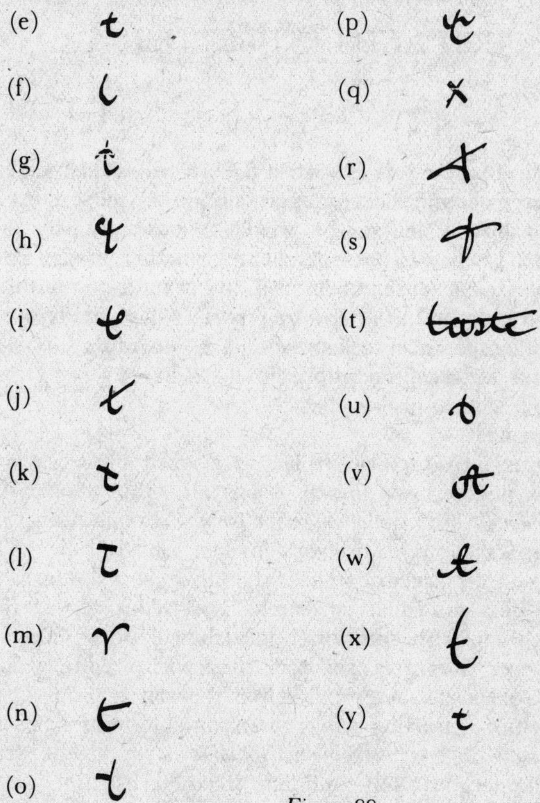

(e)	*t*	(p)	
(f)		(q)	
(g)		(r)	
(h)		(s)	
(i)		(t)	~~taste~~
(j)		(u)	
(k)		(v)	
(l)		(w)	
(m)		(x)	
(n)		(y)	*t*
(o)			

Figure 88.

Variety of Formation

Sometimes a writer will make several distinctly different *t* formations in the same script. Although such variety indicates versatility it also implies a certain inconsistency of self-control and will-power. It is not unusual for up to five or six different versions to appear and, provided that these are assessed in relationship to the rest of the sample, it is basically a question of exercising common sense when making one's analysis.

CHAPTER EIGHT

FIRST AND LAST LETTERS

The first and last letters of a written word will furnish clues to the degree of confidence or aggression in the personality; they will show whether the writer is basically shy or impulsive. They can also indicate whether a person possesses a strong sense of responsibility or tends to muddle through situations. Initial and final strokes have, therefore, a special significance in assessing an individual's basic behavioural patterns in relationships.

Initial Strokes

The various introductory strokes to a word, sentence or paragraph denote how quickly – if at all – the writer will adjust to fresh situations or react to new acquaintances, both in his social circle and work environment. Initials may be the same size, larger or smaller than the rest of the script; they can be unadorned or ornate; the writer may even embellish them with additional flourishes or underlinings. But, however they are executed, they will provide some indication of the character make-up of the writer.

An additional starting stroke to an initial letter denotes a personality who has a concern for details. Such folk are usually moderately self-confident in their attitude and approach to others.

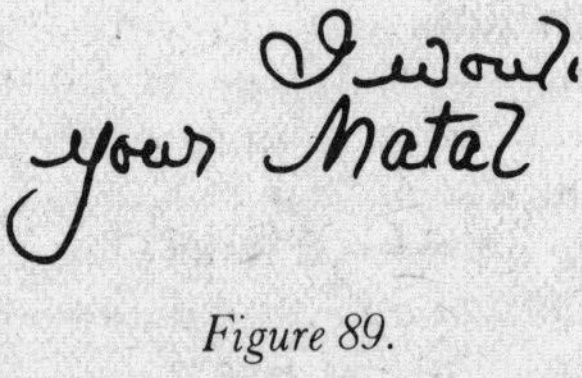

Figure 89.

These traits are exaggerated, however, when the starting strokes are long. This writer is likely to be a somewhat fussy, pernickety, over-confident individual who may well display a certain amount of aggressiveness.

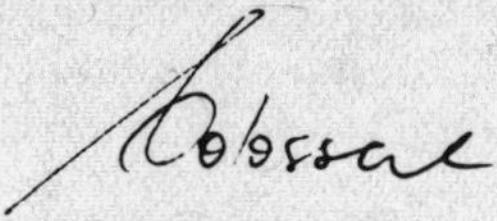

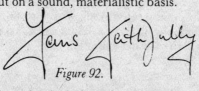

Figure 90.

When the starting stroke of a lower zone letter – such as the *g*, *p* or *y* – makes an arc formation to the left it implies a degree of self-protectiveness in the nature. These subjects tend to avoid responsibility whenever possible.

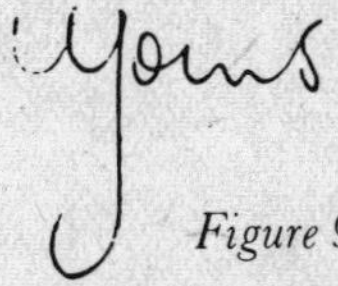

Figure 91.

However, if the lower loop of such a letter is extended to form a large triangle or has an angular appearance it is a sign of vanity. This type of person will always want everything put on a sound, materialistic basis.

Figure 92.

An upper loop that looks large in proportion to the rest of the initial letter implies that the writer is a dreamer, an idealist, perhaps even a bit of a muddler: the sort who tends to bluff his way into a situation without any clear idea of how to cope with his desired aim.

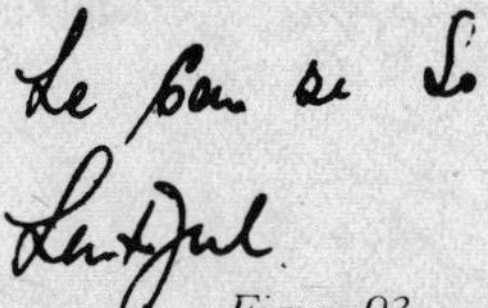

Figure 93.

When the first part of a letter such as the *m* rises upward it usually refers to a lack of confidence. These subjects tend to suffer from an inferiority complex to a lesser or greater degree and need constant reassurance and encouragement in order to counteract their inner insecurity.

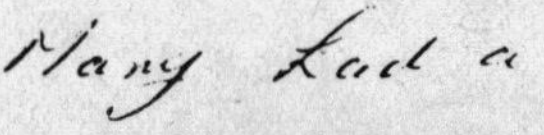

Figure 94.

Conversely, a descending initial stroke to such a letter denotes pride and arrogance. Usually, those who execute their opening strokes in such a manner have little regard for the thoughts, feelings or actions or others and tend to put their own needs and desires first.

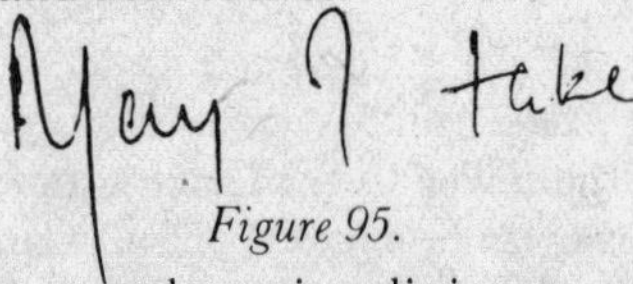

Figure 95.

Sometimes a starting letter is split into two distinct parts, implying a desire to be different from the common herd. These individuals are independent; tend to be somewhat unconventional in their thoughts and actions; and are often quite shrewd in their dealings.

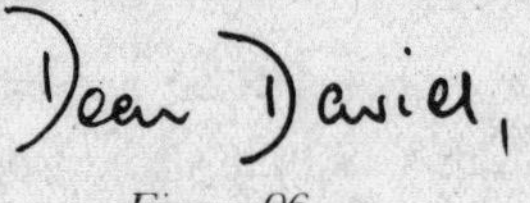

Figure 96.

Ornate initial letters can reveal a certain amount of arrogance or vulgarity in the nature. Upper zone ornamentation denotes impudence; whereas a lower zone letter emphasized in this way refers to an earthiness that could, if accentuated, prove unacceptable to others.

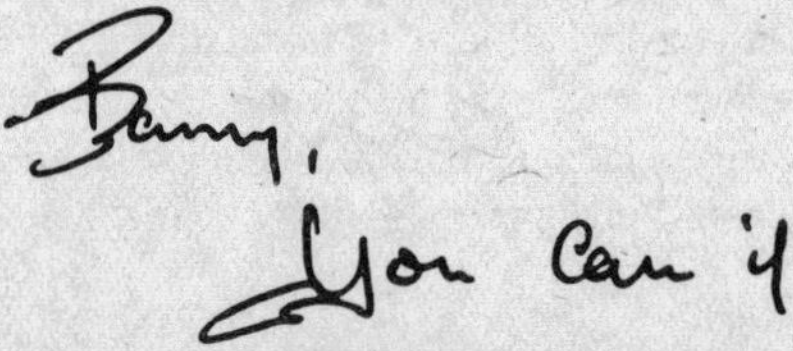

Figure 97.

Tall or thin introductory letters signify a basically shy personality. Physical shyness is implied if such a formation appears in the lower zone; in the upper zone it refers to the kind of person who often has good ideas but lacks sufficient drive to present them to others or implement them.

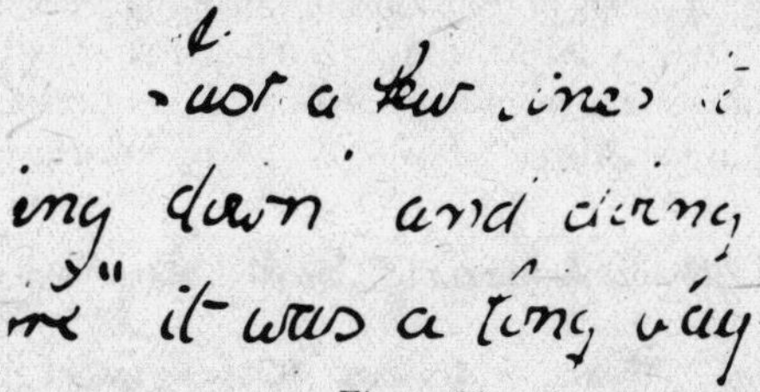

Figure 98.

A quick, penetrating mind is indicated when the initial letter lacks any additional starting stroke. Often such folk are naturally impulsive and inclined to take action without regard to future consequences.

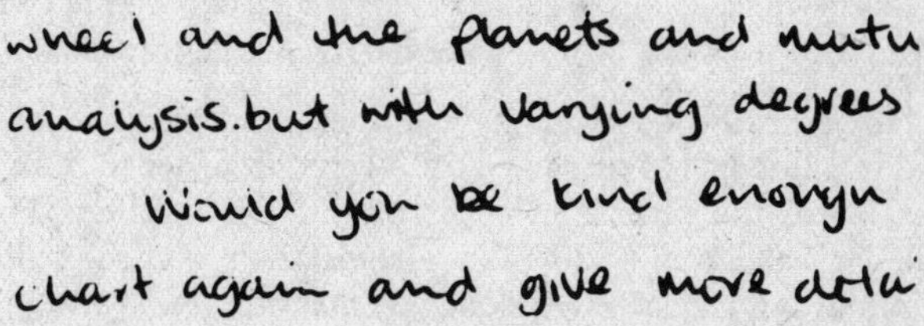

Figure 99.

Final Strokes

The last letter of a word is usually a good indicator of the level of attention employed at the time of writing. This is particularly evident with words that end sentences, lines, paragraphs and pages as these are areas where speed fluctuations are most likely to be apparent.

A clear, even script throughout a sample implies a certain level of competence; the ability to plan intelligently and the capacity to implement and maintain this quality.

Therefore, irregularities of speed and presentation will enable the student to assess the writer's powers of concentration and control.

When the evenness of a writing is reflected in the final letters of the script without recourse to extension or compression in order to maintain uniform margins, it shows that these qualities are present. Such a writer is likely to possess an adequate level of control and comprehension in all his dealings, also the ability to compromise when necessary.

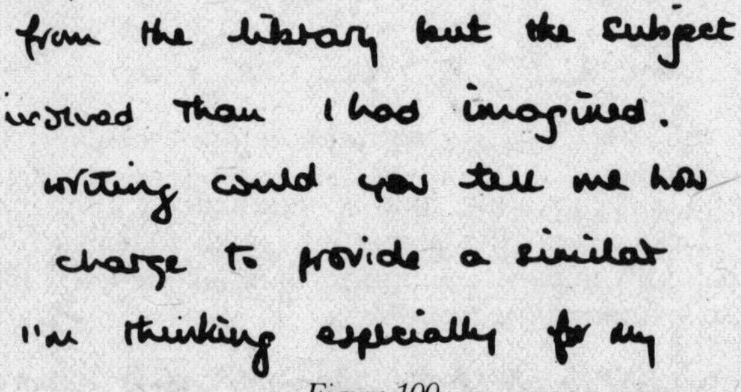

Figure 100.

However, if the writing has an uneven appearance, or the end of a line has to be raised or lowered in order to fit in the last word, the reverse of these qualities is implied. These folk lack the ability to plan ahead; their control will be minimal; and their powers of concentration weak.

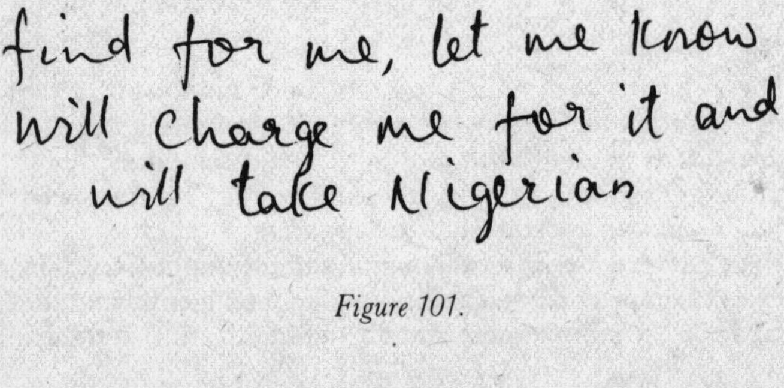

Figure 101.

If the final stroke of a word sweeps upwards, away to the left of the letter, it denotes the type of personality who tends to bend the rules to suit himself. The mood or circumstances of the moment will have priority to such a person who may well distort the truth if it serves his purpose at the time.

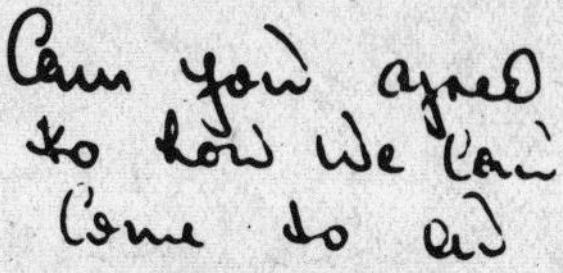

Figure 102.

An end stroke that sweeps firmly downwards under the word signifies a hot-tempered and aggressive character. These writers tend to fly off the handle with little provocation and take an uncompromising attitude in their personal relationships and business dealings.

Figure 103.

When the final flourish to a word extends horizontally to the right it implies that the writer has a generous nature. Such people are usually warm, friendly and outgoing; they have a likeable manner and create a pleasant impression on others.

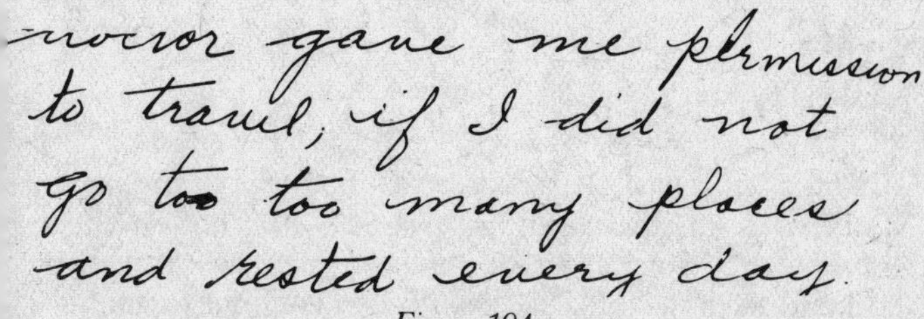

Figure 104.

However, should the last word on a line display such an exaggerated version of the above configuration that the end stroke extends to the edge of the page, it denotes fear or distrust. This type of individual may go to unnecessary extremes in order to protect property and possessions.

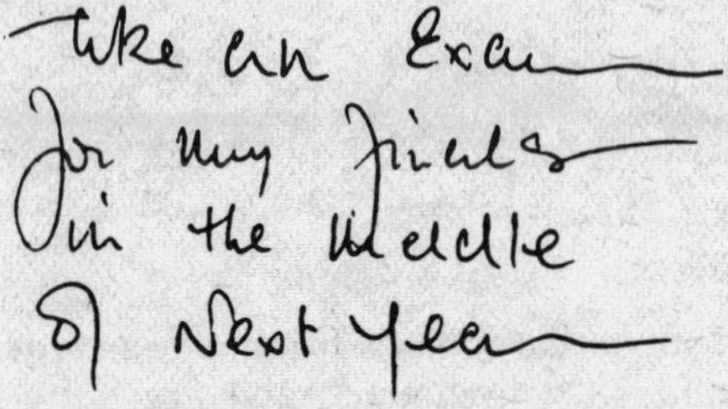

Figure 105.

A rather more common word ending is where the final stroke sweeps upwards in a curve to the right – diagonally from the base-line. This formation refers to a degree of intolerance in the overall character and, the longer the extension, the more pronounced this trait is likely to be.

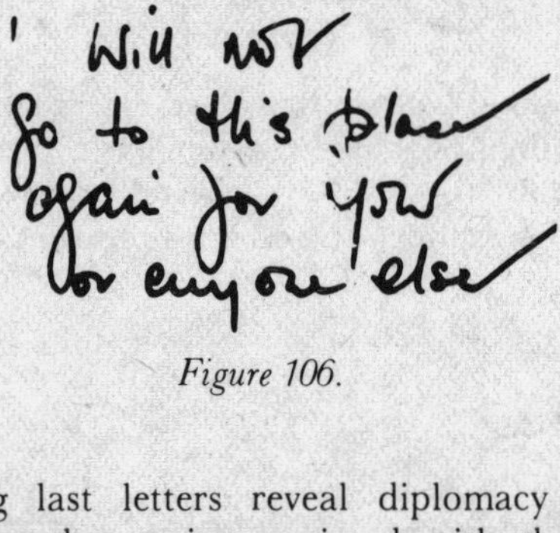

Figure 106.

Diminishing last letters reveal diplomacy and tact. Maturity is another trait associated with those writers whose words appear to decrease in size towards their termination; however, care should be taken not to confuse this style of formation with one where the final letter has a cramped or 'squeezed' appearance.

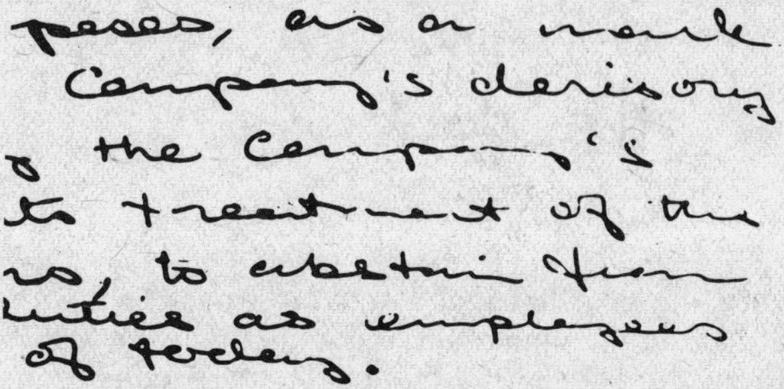

Figure 107.

The reverse configuration – where the last letter appears to grow larger – indicates a certain naivety in the personality make-up. Such people have an almost childlike simplicity; they are naturally open and frank characters.

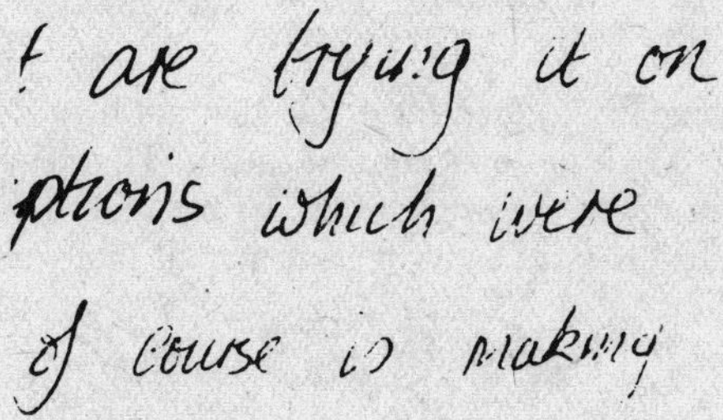

Figure 108.

A complete absence of end strokes may refer to a lack of refinement in social relationships. These individuals have a tendency to be brusque in manner and can be rather

demanding, thereby earning a reputation as somewhat
'difficult' customers.

rebel who won a
the closed shop

Figure 109.

When the final letter of a word is ornamented with a
small loop in the upper zone it signifies that the writer is
creative in some way. Such subjects are imaginative and
often utilize their creativity in artistic pursuits.

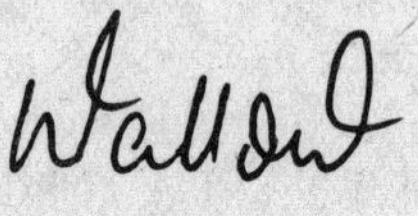

Wallow

Figure 110.

When normally looped letters – such as the *g, y, j*, or *f* –
lack a final loop it denotes concentration. The degree of this
trait is reflected by the angle of the stroke: the more vertical
the stroke the greater the writer's control is likely to be.

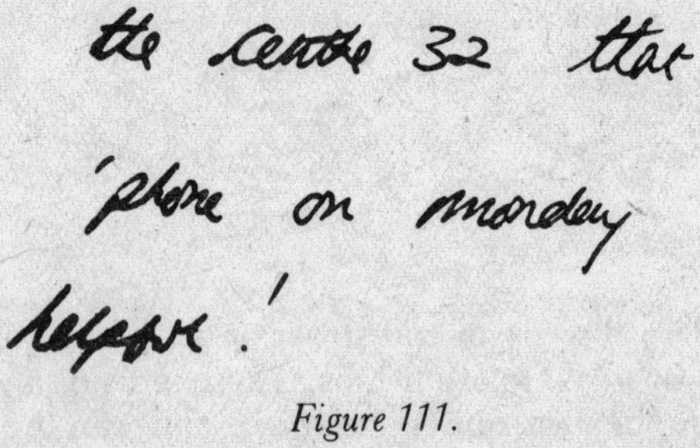

the centre 32 that

'phone on monday
before.'

Figure 111.

A triangular final loop to such letters, particularly the *g* and *y*, sometimes indicates that the writer has certain sexual problems. It may, for example, refer to a lack of sexual drive or to a physical disappointment.

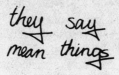

Figure 112.

A double loop in the lower part of the *g* or *y* may reflect a degree of eccentricity or affectation. Such a writer may, for instance, dress unconventionally or display odd physical mannerisms.

Figure 113.

Tiredness or physical weakness at the time of writing is quite frequently shown by end strokes that tail downwards in a script that has an overall faint or irregular appearance.

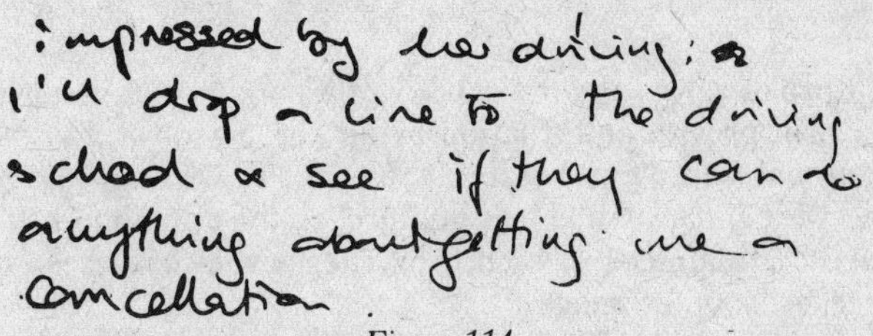

Figure 114.

Summary

Almost invariably, the beginning of a written communication will be noticeably more carefully executed than is its termination. We all set out with the very best intentions to impress the recipient but, as the writing progresses, we become increasingly absorbed in its message and decreasingly aware of ourselves: we become, in fact, less self-conscious.

The final part of a written sample will, therefore, tend to be more characteristic of our 'normal' writing than is the initial section and will reflect our true characters to a greater extent. This same principle – but to a lesser degree – can be applied to a single word: the last letter often reveals more about the writer than does the first letter because it is likely to be less consciously executed.

So, when studying a script in order to verify a character assessment, the latter parts of the sample deserve close examination. In the final analysis one should, literally, let the last letter have the last word!

CHAPTER NINE

SIGNATURES

In a broad sense, the main body of a handwritten letter or note will provide information about the person's physical, emotional and mental state at the time of writing – it will reflect the inner man. The signature, on the other hand, will reveal the manner in which the writer wishes to be seen by others – the outer image.

Often, individuals will use two different signatures, one

for business or formal letters, the other for more private or personal communications. For this reason, a certain amount of caution should be exercised when assessing a single signature, particularly if a further sample of handwriting is not available for analysis.

For obvious reasons, it is not practicable to illustrate actual signatures as examples for consideration. However, the following descriptions of the general features to observe and interpretations of their significance should aid the student graphologist.

Size

Large, bold signatures denote confident, assured personalities. This sort of individual is normally at ease in almost any environment and quite often possesses good leadership qualities. A reasonable degree of intelligence is another likely trait.

Small, insignificant signatures indicate self-consciousness. These people often lack confidence, tend to undervalue their worth and demand little recognition for their efforts. Nevertheless, they usually get along quite well when left to their own devices.

A fairly evenly balanced nature is signified by a signature that is roughly the same size as the rest of the script. Such a writer is neither pushy nor retiring, but will project his image in a quietly confident way that somehow cannot be ignored.

Legibility

A clearly legible signature is almost always a sign of sincerity and honesty in both personal and business dealings. These individuals have a nice, straightforward manner; they are discriminating, natural, outgoing and dislike fuss.

Conversely, a totally illegible signature in which even the initial letter cannot be identified implies that the writer may, literally, have something to hide. He may not keep his word despite assurances to the contrary; probably has strong reservations; and possibly fears forgery.

Curiously enough, this last-mentioned fear is unfounded. The easiest type of signature to imitate is the superficially complicated, illegible scrawl. A very simply executed signature is extremely difficult to copy with accuracy and fluidity.

Emphasis

If both forename and surname are included in a signature and are of even size it indicates a reasonable balance between the inner and outer aspects of the character. But it is, of course, not unusual for a writer to stress one part of his full name in preference to the other.

An emphasized forename implies a certain delicacy of approach. Such a writer may be subtly drawing attention to the fact that he prefers to be addressed by his full Christian name; or there may be just a hint of vanity in his nature.

When the surname is accentuated it indicates a lack of confidence and slight self-consciousness. This emphasis reflects the writer's attempt to project himself with a little more assertion than he really feels in order to impress his image on others.

Ornamentation

A much more positive indication of self-assertion is a dot after a signature. These folk are attempting to draw the attention of others to themselves and, if verified by other indications in the script, this dotting may well signify the types who will brook no opposition.

Underlining is also an attempt to emphasise the personality. A straight line underscoring the whole signature implies self-importance; a short line under the surname only signifies the writer's efforts to enhance his reputation; and a line beneath the forename only indicates his desire to draw attention to the more personal side of his nature.

Sometimes such underlining is embellished, and the greater this embellishment the more the writer is drawing attention to the self. Self-consciousness, esteem and vanity are indicated to varying degrees by the amount of ornamentation incorporated into a signature. These traits are accentuated when flourishes, twirls and curlicues ornament the initial letter, or when underlining is embellished to a noticeable extent.

Ornamental additions to a signature can reflect a love of movement and variety and should be assessed according to the zone to which they refer. Yet any form of stroke that is made above the signature, creating the impression of a roof above the names, indicates the writer's desire to protect himself from outside influences.

Other Formations

In general terms, an angular signature implies a greater degree of aggression and tension than does the softer, more rounded version of a gentler personality. Extreme aggression, in the form of rebelliousness, is sometimes indicated by a writing where the signature is crossed through.

Similarly, the overall spacing of a signature will provide a clue to the writer's basic nature. For instance, a cramped signature suggests inhibition, introversion and inner tension; a widely spaced one implies expansiveness, extroversion and release from tension.

A long starting stroke from the left can indicate that the individual is unable to rid himself of certain early memories. These sometimes develop into fixations which will influence his overall attitude and approach to others and his environment.

An end stroke to the right offers alternative interpretations according to its formation. A smooth, sweeping stroke denotes generosity; a pointed rising stroke implies aggression; and a straight, horizontal line to the edge of the page refers to defensive tendencies.

Positioning

In business communications the positioning of a signature

is often limited by the dictates of convention. But, when signing a private letter or personal note, the writer has freedom of choice in the matter and will, more often than not, automatically place a signature in a particular area on the page when at all possible.

When placed centrally beneath the main body of the writing a signature will denote the individual's desire for inner security. Such a person may be slightly diffident in manner and rather cautious in his behaviour.

These trends are accentuated if the signature is placed to the extreme left of the page. Easily disappointed and with a retiring nature, such a writer is inclined to be an escapist from reality.

Conversely, a signature to the extreme right of the page suggests a much more outgoing personality. These folk are very active, always on the go, basically love life – and fully intend to enjoy every minute of it.

Writing Styles

It is very important when considering signatures to bear in mind that these will reflect the general style of the script to a certain extent. Different countries and cultures adopt specific writing techniques which are then taught in schools as the basic 'copy-book' style of that particular system.

As people grow older, mature and develop stronger personality traits their handwriting will reflect these characteristics. Nevertheless, the script will always retain certain elements of the copy-book style taught in a particular country or educational system. It is advisable, therefore, to bear these points in mind, particularly if the signature to a handwritten sample appears to be that of a foreigner.

CHAPTER TEN

ENVELOPE ADDRESSING

Very often the first impression we receive of a writer is the one created by the manner in which he has addressed the envelope containing his communication. The way in which the name and address are written and the positioning of these in the available space will have an instantaneous visual impact on the recipient and are, therefore, worth some consideration from the graphological point of view.

Style

Frequently, the writing on an envelope is slightly different to that of the message inside. Usually it is a little larger, as though the writer is trying to boost his ego slightly; this may be due to a slight lack of self-assurance which he wishes to hide. Conversely, when the writing on the envelope is smaller than that of its contents, it may refer to a slightly false modesty; such a writer is often more self-confident than he wishes to reveal.

Out of obvious consideration for those not familiar with our personal handwriting characteristics, we should strive to make the name and address as legible as possible. Therefore, unreadable writing – particularly on an envelope – should be assessed as plain bad manners.

Many people are guilty of overlooking this small but important point and may be unaware of their lack of courtesy. It is, therefore, an indication of thoughtlessness, too. A clear-thinking, careful and considerate person will always take pains to ensure that the name and address are legible and accurate – down to the correct postcode.

Positioning

The accepted traditional position for a name and address is to place them as centrally as possible, but very few people address their envelopes in this way. However, when this information is placed firmly and squarely in the middle of the available space it denotes balance and judgement.

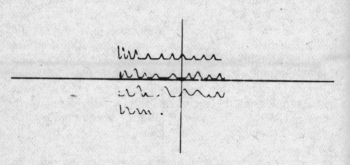

Figure 115.

An envelope addressed towards the left-hand upper corner signifies an enquiring and inquisitive mentality, but coupled with a certain degree of detachment. These writers may lack self-confidence, tend to be over-cautious and be somewhat reserved in their response to others.

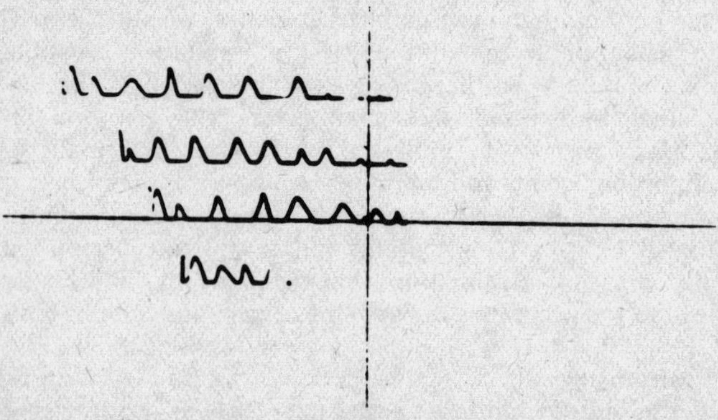

Figure 116.

These tendencies tend to be accentuated when the address appears lower down, in the bottom left-hand section of the envelope. Such folk are sometimes cautious and reserved to the point of suspicion and are likely to be somewhat materialistic in their general attitude.

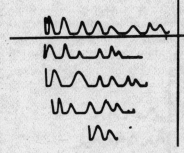

Figure 117.

Also materialistic are those writers who place the address in the bottom right-hand quarter of the envelope (*Figure 118*). These individuals are basically realistic and factual, they have few illusions, and are usually mostly concerned with the down-to-earth, practical aspects of life.

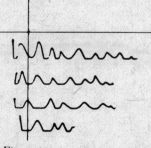

Figure 118.

An address to the top right-hand corner of an envelope denotes a desire for independence and freedom. Extroverted personalities, these writers have the ability to face future events with confidence and exhibit an open, self-assured attitude to others.

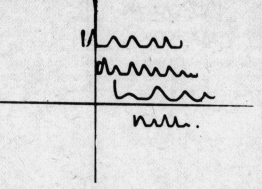

Figure 119.

Numerals

Another small pointer to the basic character of the writer is the manner in which he executes the numerals on an addressed envelope.

Clearly formed, medium sized numbers denote financial practicality; large figures, on the other hand, signify impracticality, perhaps even to the point of greed.

Numerals that are smaller than the rest of the script indicate a leaning towards the sciences. These folk are careful with finances, often have mathematical abilities, and may well take up careers in accountancy.

Those who execute badly formed figures, however, should not be trusted with other people's cash. They do not necessarily have dishonest tendencies but there is a strong likelihood that they will be careless and impractical in monetary affairs.

Any embellishment, flourishes, additional strokes or the like to the figures indicate that the writer may be suffering from some anxiety with regard to his personal financial situation at the time of writing.

First Impressions

All the points mentioned in this chapter are intended to provide quickly observable guidelines only. It is obviously impractical to undertake a detailed assessment from the information gathered from an envelope alone, although it will create an immediate, visual impression. Snap judgements should not, however, be made; a careful comparison with the handwriting of the letter or note contained is essential for a complete analysis.

INDEX